Practice and Procedure in the Master's Court

Jane Barron and Margo Ford

Practice and Procedure in
THE MASTER'S COURT

HANDBOOK FOR BARRISTERS AND SOLICITORS

WITH A FOREWORD BY

Harry Hill, SC

MASTER OF THE HIGH COURT

THE ROUND HALL PRESS

This book was typeset by
Gilbert Gough Typesetting, Dublin for
THE ROUND HALL PRESS
Kill Lane, Blackrock, Co. Dublin
and, in North America,
THE ROUND HALL PRESS
c/o International Specialized Book Services
5602 N.E. Hassalo St, Portland, Oregon 97213

ISBN 1-85800-004-1

A catalogue number for this book
is available from the British library.

Printed in Ireland by
Colour Books Ltd, Dublin

Foreword

The co-authors are to be congratulated for their legal acumen and industry in the publication of this work.

The volume of work in the Master's Court has in recent years increased greatly, and this in turn has involved more and more practitioners, both barristers and solicitors, appearing in that Court. When I commenced practice, injunctions were the preserve of the High Court or Circuit Court, but now they are regularly granted in the Master's Court; equally Discovery is now considered a vital ingredient in litigation; indeed in some cases, the Motion for Discovery has been the first intimation of litigation received by a defendant!

I wish the authors well. They deserve success with this book. It will be of great assistance to practitioners, and especially those who have recently commenced their legal careers and are perhaps making their first nervous appearances in the Master's Court.

I sincerely recommend the book to barristers and solicitors alike and especially those whose practice involves appearing in the Master's Court.

Harry Hill,
March 1994

Master's Court
Four Courts
Dublin 7.

Contents

Table of Cases

Table of Statutes and Statutory Instruments

6. European Union Legislation

1

Introduction to the Master's Court

The office of the Master of the High Court was created by the Court Officers Act, 1926, s. 3. The powers, authorities, duties and functions of the Master were set out in section 5 of that Act.

Section 31(3) of the Act of 1926 had the effect of vesting in the Master of the High Court any outstanding powers, authorities, duties and functions of statutory posts attached to the former Supreme Court of Judicature which were not otherwise allocated to holders of new posts. There is no equivalent to the Master in the Circuit or District Courts.

At the passing of the Act the Master controlled the Central Office and in addition to his general superintendence and control of the Central Office, he also exercised and had such duties and functions as were conferred on or assigned to him by statute or rule of law. In *Roe v McMullan* [1928] IR 9; 62 ILTR 33 it was held by Meredith J that the Master can only carry out the provisions of the statute or rule and that he has no specific jurisdiction. He also pointed out that if any part of the jurisdiction purported to be conferred upon the Master of the High Court by the then rules of court dealt with matters which were within 'the judicial power of the Irish Free State', the purported jurisdiction would be in contravention of Article 64 of the Constitution of Saorstát Éireann which provided that the judicial power in question should be exercised and administered in public courts established by the Oireachtas of Saorstát Éireann and by the Judges appointed. The Master of the High Court was quite clearly not a judge appointed under the Constitution of Soarstát Éireann. However, Article 37 of the Constitution of 1937 may give liberty to confer judicial function on the Master, but this has never been tested.

Until the Courts Officers Act, 1945, the Master was head of the High Court offices and superintended and controlled these. Following the Act of 1945, the Master's function was limited to dealing with matters laid down by the Rules.

The Courts (Supplemental Provisions) Act, 1961, s.14(3) provides that Rules of Court may, in relation to proceedings and matters (not being criminal proceedings or matters relating to the liberty of the person) in the High Court and the Supreme Court, authorise the Master to exercise functions, powers and jurisdiction in uncontested cases and to take accounts, conduct inquiries and make orders of an interlocutory nature.

Paragraph 4(2) of the 8th schedule of that Act sets out the powers and authorities and duties of the Master of the High Court as follows:

> The Master of the High Court shall have and exercise such powers and authorities and perform such duties and functions as are from time to time conferred on or assigned to him by statute or rules of court and in particular (unless and until otherwise provided by statute or rules of court) shall have and perform all such other powers, authorities, duties and functions as are vested in him by virtue of subsection (3) of section 31 of the Act of 1926.

As a result of *Roe v McMullan* supra and other judicial decisions the scope of the Master's jurisdiction was severely restricted and is regulated by the Rules: see *Davern v Butler* [1927] IR 182; 61 ILTR 100 and *De La Hunt v Laffan* [1927] IR 346.

FUTURE OF THE MASTER'S COURT

In the sixteenth interim report (1972) of the Committee on Court Practice and Procedure, which dealt with the jurisdiction of the Master, it was proposed that an Act of the Oireachtas should expressly confer upon the Master, jurisdiction to exercise all the authority and jurisdiction which a judge of the High Court, whether under statutory provision or otherwise, then exercised in all *ex parte* applications and in all motions on notice whether in interlocutory applications or otherwise and in all applications for judgment by consent or for judgments in default of appearance or defence except in respect of certain matters. In addition it was proposed that such legislation should enact that all the jurisdiction at that time exercised by the Master pursuant to statute or the Rules should continue to be exercised by him. Further, it was proposed that such legislation should provide that the Master might exercise such further or other jurisdiction as might from time to time be conferred by statute and that jurisdiction conferred by the Rules might be varied, rescinded or amended by subsequent rules in such a way as to have effect as if enacted by statute. The Committee also proposed that the legislation should provide for appeal to the High Court as of right in all cases in which the Master exercised jurisdiction and that there should be no restriction on the right of appeal to the Supreme Court from the decision of the High Court.

As yet none of the above proposals has been given statutory effect.

APPEALS

If a party is not satisfied with an order of the Master he may appeal to the High Court. This is done by way of Notice of Motion seeking, *inter alia*, an order setting aside the order of the Master.

The appeal motion must be issued either:

(a) within six days from the perfection (drawing up of the order by the Master's Registrar) of the Master's order, or

(b) within six days from the date of refusal by the Master, or

(c) within six days of receipt of notice of the Master's order, where the order was made *ex parte*.

In addition to this general rule regarding appeals, where an application is made to the Master pursuant to the Jurisdiction of Courts and Enforcement of Judgments (European Communities) Act, 1988 (see chapter 4) O. 42A, r. 12 provides for the lodging of an appeal by the applicant within five weeks of the date of perfection of the Master's order. Where the order is made by the Master the party against whom enforcement is made has one month (if domiciled in the State) or two months (if domiciled in another contracting state) from the date of service of the order to appeal to the High Court (O. 42A r. 11).

JUDICIAL REVIEW OF THE MASTER'S ORDER

A decision of the Master may be judicially reviewed: see *Elwyn Cottons Ltd v Master of the High Court* [1989] IR 14; wherein O'Hanlon J said at p. 16 that he was of opinion 'that an order of *mandamus* may be granted . . . requiring the Master to grant the (order) now sought'. O'Hanlon J considered the decision *The State (Gallagher, Shatter and Co.) v de Valera* (unreported, High Court, Costello J, 9 December 1983) which examined the question as to whether an order of *certiorari* could be granted by the High Court against a decision of the taxing master. O'Hanlon J accepted the decision of Costello J, in so far as it dealt with the question of making such orders against officers attached to the High Court.

APPOINTMENT OF THE MASTER

The Courts (Supplemental Provisions) Act, 1961, at paragraph 17 of the eighth schedule, provides that 'no person shall be appointed to be the Master of the High Court unless at the time of his appointment he is a barrister of not less than ten years standing who is then actually practising'.

DEPUTY MASTER

A Deputy Master may be appointed in accordance with s. 27 of the 1926 Court Officers Act. 'In the event of the temporary absence

or the temporary incapacity through illness of the Master of the High
Court . . . or in the event of the office of such Master . . . being vacant
the Minister may appoint a deputy to execute the office of such Master
. . . during such absence, incapacity, or vacancy.'

WORK OF THE MASTER'S COURT

Although the Master's jurisdiction is limited and is in many ways
administrative rather than judicial, the Master makes many of the
orders which are required prior to a full hearing in the High Court.
These include orders for discovery, interrogatories, extension of time
for various matters, directions, judgment in non-contested cases
(although the Master cannot award interest pursuant to the Courts Act,
1981). In addition the Master forwards special summonses where the
papers are in order to the appropriate Judge's list. See chapter 5 for a
detailed list of the Rules which apply to the Master and the orders he
may made.

SITTINGS OF THE MASTER'S COURT

The Master sits each day from Tuesday to Friday at 10.30 a.m. during
term time. During the long vacation the Master sits on alternate
Tuesdays.

On each day his list is set out in the Legal Diary and is divided into
several parts as follows:

1. Special Summonses: see chapter 2.

2. Motions for Judgment: see chapter 2.

3. Motions on Notice: see chapters 3 and 5.

4. Ex-parte Applications: see chapter 5.

The Tuesday, Thursday and Friday lists are divided in accordance with
1-4 above. The Wednesday list is divided similarly, but deals specifically with Family Law matters, Special Summonses under the Garda
Compensation Acts, and Revenue matters.

2

Summonses

A Special Summons is a particular type of summons which does not require pleadings as such, but the proceedings are by way of a summons with a special indorsement of claim and a grounding or verifying affidavit. In the first instance the special summons is lodged in the Central Office. At that stage it is given a Record Number for the appropriate list, e.g. court 5/6, mortgage suit, family law etc., where it will generally be heard, and it is also given a return date (O.5, rr. 4 & 5). All special summonses are returnable before the Master and the return date is fixed by the Central Office at the time of the issue of the summons.

Special summonses are dealt with in O. 3 of the Rules of the Supreme Courts 1986—'Procedure by special summons may be adopted in the following classes of claims'. To ground the jurisdiction of the Court to hear an application by special summons, the summons must disclose a cause of action of a type listed in O. 3—see *Archer v Fleming* (unreported, High Court, Finlay P, 21 January 1980). (The procedure by special summons may be adopted in virtually any matter where it is obvious that the matter can be decided on affidavit evidence.)

Order 3 sets out 21 classes of claims which may be dealt with by way of special summons procedure and O. 3(22) states that any other matter 'as the Court may think fit' may be disposed of by special summons. Once the summons is served, an appearance must be entered if the defendant wishes 'to attend and be heard' on the return date (see

Form 3 Appendix A of the Rules). In addition, O. 38 provides for the hearing of proceedings commenced by special summons. The summons must be served at least four days before the return day and an affidavit verifying the claim indorsed on the summons must be filed in the Central Office and notified to the defendant. If no service is required the return date must be not less than seven days from the date of issue of the summons (O.37, r. 1).

Special summons procedure is most commonly used for mortgage enforcement proceedings, in administration of estates, in the determination of disputes arising out of the administration of trusts and in questions of construction. It is also the means of proceeding, specified in several statutes, e.g. an appeal from the decision of the Equality Officer relating to claims brought pursuant to the Anti-Discrimination (Pay) Act, 1974; an application pursuant to the Family Home Protection Act, 1976; an application pursuant to the Succession Act, 1965. These matters come within O. 3, r. 21, and must in addition come within the jurisdiction conferred by the relevant statute in order to be heard by way of a special summons, rather than by plenary summons.

In addition O. 70A (inserted into the Rules by Statutory Instrument No. 97 of 1990, which also deleted O. 3, r. 10(c)) provides by rule 2 that *all* family law proceedings other than an application under rule 16 of that Order, shall be commenced by a special summons which shall be a family law summons. The order goes on to deal with the title of such proceedings, the contents of the special indorsement of claim and the matters to be included in the grounding or verifying affidavit (as to the contents of the special indorsement of claim on the summons pursuant to O. 70A see *H. v H.* [1991] 10 Fam LJ 6).

Following the lodgment of the Special Summons in the Central Office and prior to the return date before the Master, the grounding affidavit must be filed and a copy of the original Special Summons must be served with the grounding affidavit, at least four clear days before the return date (excluding Saturday, Sunday, Christmas Day, and Good Friday). In calculating the four days, exclude the first day, but include the last day—(see O. 122, r. 10). Thus for a Tuesday sitting of the Master's Court, the last day for service of a special summons is the previous Wednesday. If service has not been properly effected before the return date, then on the return date an application must be made before the Master to grant a new return date, as distinct from applying for an adjournment. Where only one of two defendants has been served in time, then an application can be made to the Master to adjourn against the defendant served and to seek a new return date for the defendant not served. If the Master strikes out a special summons where the plaintiff fails to appear, an application may be made to him to reinstate the summons. He may refuse to reinstate the summons, e.g. where the special indorsement of claim does not accord with the Rules—*H. v H.* [1991] (*supra*). Although O. 38, r. 5 provides that the Master may decide claims brought by special summons 'in all cases in which he shall have jurisdiction', in practice all special summons proceedings are transferred to the appropriate Judge's list for determination by the High Court.

When the matter is listed in the Master's Court, a full set of papers must be handed in to the Master, who checks that they are in order and the matter is then transferred to the Judge's List. This is done in accordance with the record number already assigned to the matter. If the special summons is in relation to a mortgage suit, being either a claim to declare a judgment mortgage well charged, or to declare a mortgage itself well charged e.g. by equitable deposit of title deeds, pursuant to the Registration of Title Act, 1964, the matter will go to that list. If it is one of a number of equity matters, e.g. injunctions, specific performance, and declaratory proceedings, it will go to one of the Chancery Court lists, at present Court 5 or Court 6.

The papers required to transfer the Special Summons proceedings to the Judge's List are:

1. The original special summons.

2. Attested and dated copy of the grounding affidavit, the original exhibits should be available to the Master, but are not actually filed

and should then be retained by the plaintiff's solicitor and handed up in the High Court, when the case comes on for hearing.

3. Notice of entry of appearance (if appearance has been entered).

4. Attested and dated copy of any replying affidavit.

5. If no appearance has been entered, an affidavit of service of the special summons.

The special summons, once put into the Judge's List, comes on for hearing before the Court on the next available Monday. The Master's only duties in relation to special summonses is to check the papers and ensure that they are in order and to transfer the matter into the appropriate list. If the papers are not in order,[1] the matter will be adjourned in the Master's List in order to get the papers in order, and the Master will not transfer the matter until he is so satisfied, whether or not it is on consent of the defendant(s). (See Rules, Appendix A Form 3 for Special Summons.) In addition to setting out the plaintiff's claim in the Special Indorsement of Claim, it is also necessary to include a schedule of affidavit or affidavits to be used by the plaintiff/applicant on the hearing of the summons.

SUMMARY SUMMONSES

Order 2 of the Rules provides for the use of Summary Summonses in various classes of claims and on consent of the parties. Proceedings commenced by summary summons are heard on affidavit, on which the deponents may be cross-examined. Once a summary summons is issued, judgment may be sought either by way of a motion for liberty to enter final judgment before the Master, or in default of appearance (in most cases) in the Central Office. (see post). When the summary

---

1. A recent practice note (5 October 1992) in relation to the Family Law list stated that the Master will not, save in special circumstances, transfer cases to the Judge's List until he is satisfied that they are ready for hearing.

summons is served the defendant has eight days within which to enter an appearance. The summons must be served on the defendant, except where the defendant by his solicitor accepts service and undertakes in writing to enter an appearance (O.9, r.1).

Summary summons procedure is most commonly used where the plaintiff is seeking to recover a debt or a liquidated demand (an amount certain, i.e an amount that is capable of being ascertained at the time of issue of the proceedings, other than damages) from a defendant who is believed not to have any defence to the action, either at law or on the merits. These types of claims are commonly brought by financial institutions, business creditors and the Revenue Commissioners. One of the advantages of proceeding by way of a summary summons is the speed with which the matter may be processed in comparison to the time taken when proceeding by plenary summons. If the plaintiff believes that he will be entitled to judgment at the stage of the motion for judgment (see below), either before the Master or the Court and that the case will not proceed to plenary hearing, then proceeding by way of summary summons will be considerably faster than commencing proceedings by way of plenary summons. The effect of bringing proceedings by way of summary summons is that the proceedings can be heard on affidavit. The deponent may be cross-examined if the other party files a notice in writing requiring the production of the deponent for cross-examination (O.37, r.2).

Order 2 provides for summary summons procedure in the following classes of claims:

> (1) in all actions where the plaintiff seeks only to recover a debt or liquidated demand in money payable by the defendant, with or without interest, arising—
> (a) upon a contract, express or implied (as, for instance, on a bill of exchange, promissory note, or cheque, or other simple contract debt); or
> (b) on a bond or contract under seal for payment of a liquidated amount of money; or

(c) on a statute where the sum sought to be recovered is a fixed sum of money or in the nature of a debt other than a penalty; or
(d) on a guarantee, whether under seal or not, where the claim against the principal is in respect of a debt or liquidated demand only; or
(e) on a trust.

In addition to debt collection, summary summons procedure may also be used by a landlord seeking to recover possession of land.

Order 2, r. 1(2) provides for the use of summary summons procedure:

> In actions where a landlord seeks to recover possession of land, with or without a claim for rent or mesne profits—
> (a) against a tenant whose term has expired or has been duly determined by notice to quit; or
> (b) for non-payment of rent.

The summary summons procedure may in addition be used in accordance with O. 2, r. 1(3), where the plaintiff in the first instance wishes to have an account taken. Therefore, the summary summons procedure may be used where the calculation of the exact sum due and owing is within the knowledge and control of the defendant (see chapter 5; O. 13, r. 17 and O. 37, r.13).

Order 2, r. 1(3) provides:

> Claims in which the plaintiff in the first instance desires to have an account taken.

Finally O. 2, r.2 states that the summary summons procedure may be adopted *by consent* of all parties in the case where the particular type of claim does not come within any of the classes in O. 2, r.1.

Order 2, r. 2 provides:

> Procedure by summary summons may be adopted by consent of all parties in the case of a claim not coming within any of the classes in rule 1.

A summary summons sets out particulars of the claim in the special indorsement of claim. The summary summons is issued in the Central Office (the original and two copies are required). The Central Office retains one of the copies. A record number is assigned to the proceedings by the Central Office at time of issue and the proceedings are assigned to a particular court list (O.5, rr. 4 & 5). The summons must then be served personally on the defendant, unless his solicitor accepts service (O.9, r.1). Where the defendant is a company service, may be by ordinary post or by leaving it at the registered office of the company (section 379 of the Companies Act, 1963).

Once served, the defendant has eight days from the date of service of the proceedings to enter an appearance. If the defendant fails to enter an appearance in time, then the plaintiff may proceed to obtain judgment in default of appearance, either in the Central Office or the Master's Court, depending on the type of claim (O.13, r.3). The summary summons procedure is therefore generally a quicker process than procedure by plenary summons, but it may only be used in the situations set out in O. 2.

As to what may be specifically indorsed, see *Bray U.D.C. v Dawson* [1938] Ir Jur Rep 66, where a right to use lands in pursuance of an agreement was held to be merely a licence to use and not a demise of the lands. It was held that a claim by the plaintiff for possession of the lands was not a claim 'for the recovery of land' within the equivalent order of the 1926 Rules of the High Court and Supreme Court, enabling such a claim to be brought by summary summons, but should have been by plenary proceedings.

In *Bank of Ireland v Lady Lisa Ireland Ltd* [1992] 1 IR 404 it was held that O.2, r.1(2) may be used in actions under section 52 of Deasy's Act (Landlord and Tenant (Ireland), Act, 1860), which permits ejectment proceedings whenever a year's rent shall be in arrear. It was further held that summary judgment will not be granted in actions for the recovery of land based on forfeiture (see also *Keating v Mulcahy* [1926] IR 214; *Meares v Connolly* [1930] IR 333); for further detail see Wylie's *Judiciature Act*, 1906 edition, pp. 190ff).

There is no power under O. 2 to hear on summary summonses issues which fall outside those listed in the Order and which ought properly to be commenced by plenary summonses: *Meares v Connolly* [1930] IR 333; see also *Bank of Ireland v Lady Lisa Ireland Ltd, supra* and *In re Hartnett; Buckley v Hartnett* [1943] IR 191, and *In re McQuillan; Meegan v Harvey* (1939) 73 ILTR 167. Further there is no power to convert a summary summons to a plenary summons, O. XV, r. 5 (of the 1926 Rules) simply allowed the court to hear a summary summons at a plenary hearing. If the wrong type of action is brought on a summary summons, the court may not amend the summary summons to a plenary summons: *Bank of Ireland v Lady Lisa Ireland Ltd* and see *Masterson v Scallan* [1927] IR 453 where it was also discussed whether the Rules are directory in nature. In that case the plaintiff's affidavit grounding the summons simply stated that the sum of money was actually due by the defendant to her, over and above all just and fair allowances. The defendants subsequently objected to the affidavit saying that it was insufficient to comply with the Rules which required an affidavit 'showing that the plaintiff is entitled to the relief claimed' to be served with the summons. The Master transferred the case to the Judge's List. Subsequently the plaintiff filed a supplemental affidavit, which showed she was entitled to the relief claimed, and upon which she relied at the hearing before the judge. The defendants contended that the failure to serve that affidavit with the summons prevented the plaintiff from recovering judgment in a summary manner under O. XV, r. 5 (1926 Rules). The Supreme Court held that the provision in the rule was directive only, and did not go to the jurisdiction, except that the affidavit mentioned must be on the record of the Court before summary judgment could be granted, and that since the plaintiff's supplemental affidavit fully established her claim, she was entitled to proceed. Fitzgibbon J held that the provision in O. XV, r. 1 (Rules of 1926) was not a condition precedent, failure to comply with which made the process a nullity, and the irregularity which existed was effectively waived by the defendants.

If there is an issue to be tried (see *post*), it will eventually be heard as if the case had commenced by the issue of plenary proceedings.

The indorsement of claim on the summary summons must state specifically the relief claimed and the grounds for the relief: see *post*.

AMENDMENT OF SUMMONSES

The decisions of *Starkey v Purfield* [1946] IR 358 and *Caulfied v Bolger* [1927] IR 117 and *Seales v McSweeney* [1944] IR 25 hold that the Master may amend special indorsements of claim, but only in conjunction with an order adjourning the matter to plenary hearing. The Master may strike out a claim or part of a claim which should not have been brought by summary summons, or may deal with part of a claim which has been correctly brought by summary summons and ignore the part of the claim which ought not have been brought by summary summons (see O.37, r.11).

In addition the summons should also contain a notice that, if the amount claimed plus the amount claimed for costs (as set out in O.4, r.5) is paid within six days after service, further proceedings will be stayed.

CONTENTS OF THE SPECIAL INDORSEMENT OF CLAIM

A Summary Summons contains a special indorsement of claim which must be clearly *particularised*: O. 4 , r.4 of the Rules states that the indorsement 'shall state specifically and with all necessary particulars the relief claimed and the grounds thereof'.

In *Allied Irish Banks Ltd v The George* (unreported, High Court, 21 July 1977) Butler J, considered and accepted the decision of Murnaghan J, in *Stacey and Harding Ltd v O'Callaghan* [1958] IR 320, where it was decided that such particulars must be given in a special indorsement of claim as may reasonably be necessary to enable the defendant to know whether he should pay or not. Particulars must be given in some detail. In the case of claims for the price of goods sold and delivered or the balance due on foot of a running account, or claims of a similar nature. Reference must also be made to the fact that full particulars have already been delivered stating the date on which and the means by which they have been furnished. It was held insufficient to state in the indorsement of claim that the claim was 'for goods sold and delivered to the defendant at the defendant's request within the last six years, detailed particulars of which said goods have already been furnished by the plaintiffs to the defendant'.

In *Caulfield v Bolger* (*supra*) it was held that a summary summons indorsed with a claim for solicitors costs, which failed to state that the bill (for the costs) had been delivered and failed to give particulars, was an insufficient indorsement.

In *Allied Irish Banks Ltd v The George* (*supra*) it was held that in the case of a claim by a bank for money owed by a customer, such as an ordinary advance or overdraft, 'it is sufficient from the point of view of pleading to claim that the money was lent and that interest at the rate normally charged by banks and bank charges have been incurred. The agreement to pay this interest and these charges may be implied. Any variation must be pleaded as an express term of the contract between the bank and the customer'.

Therefore if a plaintiff bank is seeking additional or 'penalty' interest for non-payment of a loan within an agreed time, then the relevant express term or condition should be specifically pleaded in the special indorsement of claim. In addition where there is a claim for interest arising from the agreement or under statute, it is essential to plead this specifically (see *post* for interest).

In *McMullan Brothers Ltd v Ryan* [1958] IR 94 it was held that there was no requirement that a special indorsement of claim should contain a statement that statutory requirements had been complied with: such details would not come within the meaning of 'the relief claimed' or 'the grounds thereof'.

That case dealt with a claim for arrears of rentals due under a hire-purchase agreement. It is provided in the Hire Purchase Act, 1946, that section 3 thereof must be complied with prior to entitlement to relief under the Act. This situation is now specifically dealt with by O. 4, r. 13 (which provides that the special indorsement of claim shall state that the statutory requirements pursuant to section 3 have been complied with).

The following are examples of classes of claim which may be made on a summary summons:

Guarantees The special indorsement in guarantee claims must set out:

(a) the details of the guarantee and that the guarantor agreed to pay to the plaintiff either a maximum sum or an unlimited amount where the principal debtor defaults;

(b) the fact that a demand was made on the guarantor and the method of such demand;

(c) the date of demand.

Simple interest may be claimed in addition to the principal sum from the date of demand.

Bank loans Where a claim is made by a bank the special indorsement of claim must specify:

(a) the loan agreement and terms thereof, in particular relating to interest payments (see *Allied Irish Banks Ltd v The George, supra*);

(b) the principal sum due, as of the last rest day (i.e. the day when the interest was last compounded with the principal);

(c) the date of the relevant rest day;

(d) additional amount of (simple) interest accumulated to the date of issue of the proceedings (from rest date);

(e) claim for simple interest to date of judgment.

This method of making a claim means that the parties can ascertain the amount payable by the defendant at the date of issue of the proceedings. If compound interest was claimed then the sum due and owing would no longer be ascertainable and therefore would not come within Order 2 r.1.

Revenue/tax Many revenue claims are dealt with by way of Summary Summons procedure. In particular claims for unpaid tax e.g. VAT, PRSI and PAYE. The special indorsement of claim in these cases must set out:

(a) the sum due;

(b) how it became due, e.g. by virtue of assessments;

(c) that a demand was made, and how made;

(d) that the sum due still remains unpaid.

The claim seeks the principal and interest outstanding as of the date of the issue of proceedings. The revenue authorities are entitled to claim 1.25% penalty interest per month for non-payment of tax (Income Tax Act, 1967, s. 550).

Goods sold and delivered These type of claims are made by creditors who have not been paid for goods. It is essential to set out in the special indorsement of claim:

(a) the dates on which the goods were sold and delivered;

(b) that the goods were delivered at the defendant's request;

(c) that all the goods were delivered within the last six years;

(d) if interest is claimed, the agreement to pay interest must be specifically pleaded.

When the details in the summary summons are insufficient to show that the plaintiff is entitled to the relief claimed then judgment should not be given on it—*O'Gorman v Long* (1959) 93 ILTR 3—and '. . . where a plaintiff proceeds by summary summons he must not only plead a cause of action which under the rules may be brought by summary summons but must support his claim by evidence. If such evidence is not forthcoming the action should be dismissed' *per* Lavery J in *Bond v Holton* [1959] IR 302.

If the particulars of the special indorsement of claim are shown to be incorrect, it is not possible to amend or cure them by affidavit, and therefore the plaintiff will have to start again. If the particulars are correct, but the affidavit is incorrect, then a new motion may be brought with a new affidavit: see *Allied Irish Banks Ltd v The George* (*supra*).

WHERE THE DEFENDANT ENTERS AN APPEARANCE

Where no appearance is entered the plaintiff may adopt the procedure set out in O. 13 (Default of Appearance) and apply for judgment in the Central Office (see *post*: chapter 5 and appendices).

Where the defendant enters an appearance to the summary summons then the plaintiff continues as follows:

MOTION ON NOTICE SEEKING LIBERTY TO ENTER FINAL JUDGMENT

The plaintiff pursues his claim by bringing a motion on notice before the Master of the High Court seeking *liberty to enter* final judgment for the relief claimed in the summary summons together with interest and costs. Where the Master makes the order sought, this permits the plaintiff to enter final judgment in the Central Office at a later stage.

1. Procedure

(a) The motion must be served *at least four clear days* before the date fixed for the hearing of the motion (O.37, r.1). In calculating '4 clear days' Saturday, Sunday, Christmas Day and Good Friday must be excluded (see O.122, rr. 2 and 10). The practice in the Central Office is to give a return date of approximately 10 days after issue of the notice of motion.

(b) In addition the motion must be grounded on an *affidavit*, to be served with the notice of motion, sworn by or on behalf of the plaintiff.

(c) The affidavit sworn by or on behalf of the plaintiff must show firstly a *prima facie* case, that he is entitled to the relief claimed and secondly must state that it is the deponent's belief that the defendant has no defence to the action (O.37, r.1). However, see *Masterson v Scallan* (*supra*) where it was held that the affidavit grounding the application must be on the Court record before summary judgment will be granted. The affidavit must be sworn by a person who can swear positively to the relevant facts, e.g. the bank manager (O.31, r.1). See *Frederici v Vanderzee* (1877) 2 CPD 70. Where the claim is one by a bank or other financial institution the affidavit should include interest calculations up to the date of the swearing of the affidavit and should contain an averment to the effect that interest continues to accrue until judgment is entered or until payment. This is necessary because interest rates may vary at any time and it is, therefore, impossible to calculate the exact sum in advance.

2. Reply

After receipt of the motion, should the defendant wish to defend the proceedings, he must file a replying affidavit disclosing a defence and serve a true copy of same on the plaintiff (O.37, r.3). The affidavit

sworn by the defendant or on the defendant's behalf if the defendant
is a company, must show that there is a good defence on the merits, or
by disclosing such facts as may be deemed sufficient to entitle him to
defend: see Wylie (*supra*). The defendant may show cause against
such motion by offering to bring the sum of money indorsed on the
summons into court (O.37, r.3). The affidavit must contain more than
the statement that the defendant has a good defence: see *Anon* (1875)
WN 249, *per* Quain J at p. 250: 'A mere affidavit that the defendant
has a good defence is not sufficient ground for refusing to allow
judgment to be signed under this Rule. That would be encouraging
defendants to make illusory affidavits'; see also *Wallingford v Mutual
Society* (1880) 5 App Cas 685. There must be a *bona fide* defence or
an issue raised against the claim which ought to be tried.

If the affidavit has not been filed and served by the time the motion
comes on for hearing before the Master, the Master will usually
adjourn the motion to allow the defendant time to file and serve such
an affidavit.

3. Hearing of the motion

When the motion finally comes on for hearing before the Master, the
plaintiff will require the following documents, which are essential
proofs for a motion seeking liberty to enter final judgment before the
Master, and must be handed in to the Master:

(a) Original summons and appearance;

(b) Notice of Motion together with an affidavit of service of the notice
of motion and the grounding affidavit;

(c) Certified copy of grounding affidavit together with original exhibits, if any;

(d) Certified copy of replying affidavit together with original exhibits,
if any.

If the defendant files and serves a replying affidavit, the Master may make one of the four following orders:

(i) Where the matter is a contested one, he must transfer the motion to the Judge's list (O.37, r.6). The Master is obliged to transfer any contested case, i.e where the defendant has shown cause in his replying affidavit, to the Judges's List on the following or next available Monday, unless the parties consent to go for plenary hearing (see *post*).

Where the replying affidavit discloses a potential defence the Master will transfer either the whole of the matter to the Judge's list, or if it discloses a potential defence to only part of the matter, he may give liberty to enter final judgment for the part of the claim for which no potential defence is disclosed (or for the undisputed part of the relief claimed), and transfer the remainder of the claim to the Judge's list, or give judgment for the balance where the defendant has made part payment.

Having made such an order, the Master may also grant liberty to file further affidavits before the Court hearing (O.37, r.6).

In addition, the Master may adjourn or transfer the motion to the Judge's list where there is interest sought, pursuant to section 22 of the Courts Act, 1981 (O.37, r.5).

(ii) The Master may adjourn the matter to plenary hearing—This must be done on consent of all the parties (O.37 r.6). Where this is done, the Master may give directions as to the pleadings to be filed and orders for discovery, and settlement of issues to be tried (O.37, r.6).

If it appears from the grounding and replying affidavit that there is a conflict of evidence relating to the facts which are relevant to the outcome of the case, it may be advisable for the parties to ask the Master to adjourn the case to plenary hearing.

(iii) Where the plaintiff has no case, the Master may dismiss the claim and refuse to give liberty to enter final judgment—see Wylie (*supra*).

(iv) If the replying affidavit clearly reveals no defence then the

Master may make the order sought (giving liberty to enter final judgment): see *Thompson v Marshall* (1880) 28 WR 220; *Wallingford v Mutual Society* (*supra*). Where the defence is purely for the purpose of delay: see *Lloyd's Banking Co. v Ogle* (1876) 1 Ex D 262 (see Wylie, *supra*).

The merits of the case are not to be gone into at the hearing of the motion before the Master: see *Jacobs v Booth's Distillery* (1901) 50 WR 49. In that case, which dealt with O. 14 of the Rules then in force, the Earl of Halsbury LC stated at page 49 that this rule was 'intended to prevent sham defences from defeating the rights of the parties by delay, and at the same time causing great loss to plaintiffs who were endeavouring to enforce their rights'. Lord James of Hereford also stated at page 49, that the question which should be asked is: 'Is there a triable issue to go before a jury or court?' Where there is any doubt the motion should be refused and the defendant be entitled to defend the action: see *Thompson v Marshall* (*supra*).

In *Munster and Leinster Bank Ltd v Coffey* (1940) 74 ILTR 84 it was held that in deciding whether to adjourn a case to plenary hearing the court should have regard to whether the plaintiff appears to be entitled to the relief sought and whether any defence is disclosed. If the plaintiff's affidavit established that he was entitled to the relief sought and the defendant's affidavit did not give rise to any facts that might raise a defence, the case should not go for plenary hearing. The proper course would be to grant the relief sought by the plaintiff.

In *Irish Dunlop Co. Ltd v Ralph* (1958) 95 ILTR 70 it was held that the defendant having disclosed facts constituting a good *prima facie* answer to the plaintiff's claim the action should be allowed to go forward for plenary hearing. The defendant's claim was connected with the subject-matter of the plaintiff's claim and both claims could be dealt with together at plenary hearing. 'Both claims, plaintiffs' and defendant's arise out of the relationship of landlord and tenant, and the defendant's claim, in my opinion, clearly falls into the category of an equitable set-off and is proper to be allowed to be advanced in an answer to the plaintiff company's claim. It may, moreover, be observed that so far as the affidavits go the defendant's claim for damages for breach of covenant stands uncontroverted', *per* O'Daly J at p. 76.

In *Codd v Delap* (1905) 92 LT 510 it was held that leave should not be given to enter final judgment where a real and substantial question was to be tried.

EVIDENCE AT THE HEARING OF THE MOTION FOR LIBERTY TO ENTER FINAL JUDGMENT

The motion for liberty to enter final judgment is usually heard on affidavit, but either party can in advance of such motion seek to have the other side's deponent cross-examined before the Master. Order 37, r.2 requires that a notice in writing requiring the production of the deponent for cross-examination be served upon the other party. If the deponent is not produced, the relevant affidavit is inadmissible as evidence, unless special leave is given by the Master. If necessary a *subpoena* may issue from the Central Office for the attendance of a witness before the Master provided that the Master approves same in advance (O.39, r.27).

The Master has full power to summon parties and witnesses to attend before him and to require the production of documents (O.63, r.8).

HEARING OF UNCONTESTED CASES—OR WHERE NO DEFENCE SHOWN

Where the motion is uncontested then the Master may deal with the matter summarily. He may grant liberty to enter final judgment where the defendant files an affidavit where there is clearly no defence (see above).

The affidavit on which the motion is grounded must be full. It must explain the background and must show any changes in the amount claimed since the date of issue of the summons. One paragraph of the affidavit should set out the total amount claimed including any additional interest accrued, and any payments made where the total differs from that on the indorsement of claim.

Pursuant to O. 37, r.12, in any case of difficulty or doubt, the Master may transfer the case to the court list for hearing notwithstanding that he might have had jurisdiction to deal with the case himself under this order. He may do this where there is consent to enter judgment in a higher sum than that claimed.

ACCOUNTS AND INQUIRIES

Order 37, r.13 deals with summary summonses seeking inter alia the taking of an account. Where the defendant fails to appear the Master shall make such an order. Only accounts and inquiries which are subsidiary to determining the rights of the parties may be directed— *Garnham v Skipper* (1885) 29 Ch D 566—see chapter 5. Such accounts and inquiries cannot be directed by the Central Office in default of appearance, but on foot of a notice of motion and affidavit (sworn after the time for entering an appearance has expired) and must state concisely the grounds of the plaintiff's claim to an account, and the accounts required. When the defendant does appear accounts are dealt with by the High Court and not by the Master.

HEARING IN THE HIGH COURT

When the matter comes on in the Judge's List. the Court may give judgment in full or in part or may dismiss the action or may adjourn the case to plenary hearing as if the proceedings had been commenced by plenary summons. The Court may also give directions as to further pleadings, discovery, and the settlement of the issues to be tried at plenary hearing (Order 37, r.7).

GETTING INTEREST IN THE MASTER'S COURT

Only a judge of the High Court may award interest pursuant to the Courts Act, 1981. Such interest cannot be granted, either where judgment is given in default of appearance in the Central Office, or by virtue of the Master's order for liberty to enter final judgment.

Therefore, if a plaintiff claims this interest in his proceedings, he must waive it to get judgment in these circumstances. This was decided in the case of *Mellohide Products Ltd v Barry Agencies Ltd* [1983] ILRM 152. The Courts Act, 1981 states that a Judge may award interest, and it was held that neither the High Court Registrar nor the Master of the High Court is a judge for this purpose.

Therefore, if the plaintiff wishes to pursue his claim for interest pursuant to the Courts Act, 1981, he must issue a motion for judgment to the Master of the High Court and have it transferred to the Judge's List. Then when the matter comes before a judge of the High Court, the judge may make the order and award interest. The interest runs from the date of accrual of the debt to the date of judgment. In addition the plaintiff is entitled to interest from the date of judgment. Since 23 January 1989 the interest rate has been 8%.

Order 37, r.5 specifically deals with the fact that the Master cannot award interest pursuant to the Courts Act, 1981: either the plaintiff must waive the claim to interest under the Courts Act, 1981 and the Master can then give liberty to enter final judgment for the principal sum claimed only. Alternatively if the plaintiff wishes to continue with his claim for interest, the whole matter may be transfered to the judges list: see further O. 13, r.19, which permits an *ex parte* application to be made to the Court, where judgment would otherwise be entered in the Office. In this case, the Court will make the order for judgment for the full amount plus interest.

FOREIGN CURRENCY

The Master can give liberty to enter final judgment in a foreign currency, if the summary summons is so indorsed and judgment can be entered in the Central Office for such foreign currency sum. If the sum is converted, it should be converted at the official exchange rate, as of the date of when the judgment in default is entered in the Central Office, not at the date of the Master's order: see *Damen v O'Shea* [1976-77] ILRM 275.

Where the Master gives liberty to enter final judgment, then the Order states that the plaintiff is to be entitled to enter judgment in the Central Office. Therefore, to obtain judgment, the plaintiff must apply to the Central Office, as with judgment in default. The papers required are:

(a) copy of the Master's Order. This may include an order that the plaintiff is entitled to interest from the date of the Master's Order to the date of entering judgment in the Central Office.

(b) a judgment form—similar to the one used for judgment in default. In addition to the standard matters to be set out therein, it must also include the terms of the Master's Order.

(c) a supplemental affidavit may be required, which would set out the interest, from the date when the Master gave liberty to enter final judgment to the date of judgment.

Again as with judgment in default in the Central Office the Registrar of the Central Office signs the judgment form. Should the defendant pay part of the sum owed, between the time of the Master's order and the time of applying to enter final judgment, then judgment can only be entered for the balance.

JUDGMENT IN DEFAULT IN THE CENTRAL OFFICE

To obtain judgment in the Central Office, the plaintiff must lodge the required documentation known as a 'judgment set', this includes:

(a) the original summons with service endorsed. Service must be endorsed within three days of serving the summons on the defendant. If the summons is not endorsed within time, an application may be made to the Master to extend the time to endorse service: see chapter 5;

(b) a grounding affidavit, also known as an affidavit of debt. This affidavit should set out in full the sum owing to the plaintiff by the defendant (O.13, r.18). Where the claim is one by a bank or other financial institution, the affidavit should clearly set out the interest calculations based on the principal as stated in the special in-dorsement of claim;

(c) an affidavit of service;

(d) a judgment form setting out the amount due and owing by the defendant as of the date of swearing the grounding affidavit;

(e) in addition, where the claim is for recovery of land based on non-payment of rent, the landlord or his agent must make and file an affidavit stating that there was at the date of commencement of the proceedings at least one year's rent due over and above all just and fair allowances (O.13, r.4): see chapter 5.

If all the documents are in order the Judgment Form is signed by the Registrar in the Central Office and the plaintiff then has judgment as of that date. The plaintiff may then proceed to execute on foot of this judgment, in the usual manner.

There are two exceptions to proceeding to judgment in the Central Office, when it becomes necessary to apply to the Master for judgment in default of appearance. The exceptions are in relation to Hire Purchase Agreements and claims by a moneylender—leave must first be obtained from the Master (O.13, r.3): see chapter 5.

Where judgment in default is sought in the Central Office in cases other than for a liquidated demand, e.g. recovery of land, the plaintiff may proceed to enter judgment for possession but the order will not provide for the plaintiff's costs. However, the plaintiff may have his costs taxed and pursue a separate claims for such costs, once they have been ascertained.

Where the defendant has not entered an appearance within the 8 days from the date of service of the summons and the plaintiff fails to proceed to get judgment in default, the defendant may still enter an appearance. The Rules provide that the defendant may enter an appearance at any time prior to the date of judgment. This does not apply in the case of actions for the recovery of land—O. 12, r.13, except with the permission of the Court: see chapter 5.

3

Pre-trial Procedures

DISCOVERY, INSPECTION AND INTERROGATORIES

The origins of the pre-trial procedures lie in the equitable jurisdiction of the Courts of Chancery and Exchequer. The term 'Discovery' once encompassed what are now known as Discovery, Inspection and Interrogatories. 'The function of discovery of documents is to provide the parties with the relevant documentary material before the trial so as to assist them in appraising the strength or weakness of their respective cases, and thus to provide the basis for the fair disposal of the proceedings before or at the trial' (*per* Halsbury's Laws of England, 4th edition) and in this way eliminates surprise at or before the trial relating to documentary evidence and reduces the costs of the litigation. 'The purpose of discovery is to provide, by means of this pre-trial procedure, against unfair evidential advantage being taken at the trial': *per* Henchy J at p. 129 *McCarthy v O'Flynn* [1979] IR 127. For these reasons an application will be refused, if the Master forms the opinion that no order is necessary 'either for disposing fairly of the cause or matter or for saving costs' (O.31, r.12(3)).

DISCOVERY

An application for an order for discovery is made when a party to legal proceedings seeks disclosure by another of the existence of documents which the latter has or has had in his possession, power or procurement which are relevant to the matters in issue between the parties (O.31, r.12). In probate, admiralty actions and matrimonial petitions the Master may on a motion for directions grant amongst other orders, an order for discovery (O.36, r.4)

Procedure   Letter requesting voluntary discovery
Notice of motion
2 clear days' notice
4 clear days for personal service

Proofs   (a) Notice of motion
(b) Affidavit of service of (a) and (b)
(c) Copy pleadings
(d) Name of intended deponent [Note: the Master will not make an order until he has been supplied with such name.]

Pre-application procedure Under O. 31, r. 12(4) it is necessary to make prior written application seeking voluntary discovery, to the party or person against whom discovery is sought. A reasonable period of time for such voluntary discovery should be allowed before proceeding with a motion for discovery. The Rules contain a proviso that the Court may, where the matter is urgent, or with the consent of the parties, or for any other valid reason, make such order as appears proper, without the necessity for such prior written application.

Where voluntary discovery is sought and agreed it shall be in like manner and form and have such effect as if directed by order of the Court. The other party or person must be informed at the time of the application that such application is being made in accordance with O. 31, r. 12(4) and if they agree to make discovery, it must be made in like manner and form and will have effect as if directed by Court order. They must also be informed that failure to make such agreed discovery may result in an application for attachment pursuant to O. 31, r. 21. The applicant may also apply pursuant to O. 31, r. 21 to have other party's action dismissed for want of prosecution where they are plaintiff or to have the other party's defence struck out where they are defendant.

Time for making voluntary discovery of documents   Pursuant to O. 31, r. 12(4)(4) an application for discovery under O. 31, r. 12(1) or (4) shall be made not later than 28 days after the action has been set down or in matters which are not set down 28 days after it has been listed for trial. This time limit may be extended by agreement between the parties or by order of Court where it appears just and reasonable to do so.

Before an order for discovery will be made, the issues between the parties must be clearly defined. It follows that although the Master has jurisdiction to make an order for discovery at any time, subject to O. 31, r. 12(4), such order would not normally be granted to a plaintiff before he has filed his statement of claim, nor to a defendant before he has filed his defence. Although pre-pleading discovery is allowed under the rules, exceptional circumstances would have to be shown to ground a successful application. In an application to the court for an interlocutory injunction, where an order for discovery is sought, an argument that in practice a decision on such interlocutory application is often conclusive, will not provide sufficient grounds for an order of discovery to be made at that stage: see *R.H.M Foods Ltd v Bovril Ltd* [1982] 1 All ER 673.

But a defendant may for example, be granted discovery where it is almost certain that a defence of a particular nature will be raised and the discovery is only for the purpose of enabling the defendant to plead his defence with greater particularity.

Type of order sought by applicant   In his notice of motion the applicant may seek a general order for discovery seeking for example 'all relevant documents in the possession, power and control of the respondent his servants or agents' between the dates in question. An applicant may alternatively seek a limited order listing the nature and categories of the documents he wants the respondent to discover.

Meaning of 'documents' 'Documents' under O.31, r.12 include X-ray photographs and plates, *McCarthy v O'Flynn* [1979] (*supra*) and may include a computer database, *Derby & Co. Ltd v Weldon (No. 9)* [1991] 1 WLR 652, as it contains information capable of being retrieved and converted into a readable form.

Documents must be 'relevant' Discovery may be ordered of any document which might reasonably be supposed to contain information which would advance the case of one party or damage that of the other. This test of relevancy was laid down in *Sterling Winthop Group Ltd v Farben Fabriken Bayer A.G.* [1967] IR 97 and was approved and applied by the Supreme Court in *Dunne v National Maternity Hospital* (unreported, Supreme Court, 31 October 1989).

Effect of an order for discovery An order for discovery does not, of itself oblige production of the documents in question (see Inspection, pp. 36ff *infra*). The respondent is obliged to discover on oath (i.e. to make a complete sworn list) all 'relevant' documents which come into his possession both before and after the Order is made.

Hearing of an application for discovery before the Master The Master has jurisdiction to refuse or adjourn a discovery application, if satisfied that such discovery is not necessary or not necessary at that stage of the cause or matter (O.31, r.12(1)) i.e. necessary for the fair disposal of the action. See *Dolling-Baker v Merrett & Ors* [1991] 2 All ER 890. Alternatively he may make an order to alter or limit the discovery sought, or make an order on such terms as to security for the costs of the discovery as he may think fit (O.31, r.12(1).) The Master also has power to order that the respondent, in lieu of filing an affidavit, deliver to the applicant a list of relevant documents which are or have been in his possession custody or power. Should the Master make such an Order he is not thereby precluded from later ordering the making and filing of an affidavit of documents. The Master may also grant a cross order (thereby also ordering the applicant to make discovery).

Costs The Master may make any order as to the costs of the application. O.31, r.25 provides that the costs shall be allowed as part of the costs of the applicant unless otherwise ordered by the Court. Where an order for discovery is made, the usual order reserves the question of costs. The costs may then be awarded as part of the costs of the action. Where an application is made without the prior request in writing for voluntary discovery or after the time allowed for such an application, the costs 'shall be in the discretion of the Court' (O. 31, r.12(4).

Form of the affidavit of discovery of documents The affidavit of discovery should be in the form set out in the Rules at No. 10, Appendix C, Affidavit as to Documents (O.31, r.13).

Grounds of objection to making discovery The following list is not intended to be exhaustive as the grounds of objection will lie in the facts of each case,

(a) Discovery is unnecessary or premature (O.31, r.12.3.) The respondent may argue that the applicant is merely engaging in a 'fishing expedition' (*Shaw v Vauxhall Motors Ltd* [1974] 2 All ER 1185).

(b) That the applicant's entitlement to discovery is dependant upon the determination of an issue or question in dispute in the cause or matter, or that such determination is desirable before deciding upon discovery. The Master may order such determination and adjourn the discovery application or put the matter into the Court list at the request of one of the parties.

(c) The respondent does not have any relevant document or the documents the discovery of which is being sought, in his possession, power or control.

(d) Discovery is being sought of documents which are not relevant (*Dunne v National Maternity Hospital, supra*).

A claim to privilege is not a good ground of objection to discovery but may be claimed in the affidavit of discovery itself in order to resist inspection. Where such a claim is made and a serious dispute exists between the parties on the issue of privilege the Master may be requested by one of the parties to put the matter into the Court list.

Further and better discovery   If the Master limits the discovery sought, or the applicant is otherwise dissatisfied with the discovery made by the respondent, he may seek further and better discovery after the Master's order has been complied with. A grounding affidavit is required showing why a further order is necessary: see *Bula Ltd (in receivership) v Crowley* [1990] ILRM 756, [1991] IR 220, for principles to be applied, *Bord na Mona v John Sisk & Son Ltd* [1990] IR 85 and *O'Leary v Minister for Industry & Commerce* [1966] IR 676).

Appeal   An appeal may be taken to the High Court against an order of the Master within six days of the date of perfection of the Master's order (i.e. the date the order is signed by the Master's Registrar). Such appeal is made by way of motion on notice (O.63, r.9.)

Failure to comply with an order for discovery   Should any party fail to comply with an order for discovery, O.31, rr.21-23 set out the potential consequences. If the party in default is the plaintiff, he is liable to have his action dismissed for want of prosecution, if the defendant, his defence may be struck out and he may be placed in the same position as if he had not defended. Where a party fails to make voluntary discovery as agreed, an application may be made under O. 31, r. 21. On such an application the Court may, if satisfied that it is proper so to do, make such order under rr. 12, 19 and 21 as is appropriate or such other order as appears just in the circumstances.

O.31, r.21 also states that failure to comply with an order for discovery renders the party in default liable to attachment. Default applications must be made by way of motion on notice to the High Court. Non-compliance with an order for discovery does not relieve an applicant of his obligations under a cross order made against him.

A solicitor may find himself liable to attachment where an order for discovery has been served upon him and he has failed, without reasonable excuse, to notify his client of his obligations under the order. He must also warn his client to protect against the eventuality of damage to, destruction or loss of any relevant document (O.31, r.23.).

Inspection of the documents—see Section B Inspection will normally follow as a matter of course from an order for discovery when production of the documents listed in the schedules of the affidavit of discovery is requested, and copies may be taken. If an objection is raised it will then be necessary to make application to the Master for an order of inspection.

Third-party discovery O.31, r.29 governs third party Discovery against any person who is not a party to the proceedings. Before any application is made the applicant should seek voluntary discovery (see above). An applicant for such an order must provide the Master with sufficient evidence to show that the relevant documents are or are likely to be in the possession, power or procurement of the respondent. An unsupported averment to that effect will be inadequate. Under r. 29 the Court has a discretion in the making of such an order and must have evidence on affidavit from which it can conclude that

(a) the relevant documents exist (i.e., documents which are relevant to an issue likely to arise at the hearing of the action) and

(b) that it is *likely* that the third party has the relevant documents in his possession power or procurement: see *Holloway v Belenos Publications* [1987] ILRM 790; *O'Connell v RTE* (unreported, High Court, Blayney J, 2 November 1988); and also *A.I.B. v Ernst and Whinney* [1993] 1 IR 375.

The party seeking an order under O.31, r.29 must indemnify the third party making discovery in respect of all costs reasonably incurred by him in complying with such order. In *Holloway v Belenos Publications and others* [1988] IR 494; the high court held that the power of the court to order discovery against a third party was part of the inherent jurisdiciton of the court.

Procedure   Letter requesting voluntary discovery
Motion on notice
2 clear days' notice
4 clear days for personal service

The notice of motion should be served on all parties to the action unless it is clear that a party does not wish to be heard (*per* Costello J, *Holloway v Belenos Publications* supra at p. 796).

Proofs: (a) Notice of motion
(b) Grounding affidavit (essential)
(c) Affidavit of service of (a) and (b)
(d) Copy pleadings
(e) Name of intended deponent

If an order is made for third party discovery the same consequences flow from that order as if it was made inter partes.

INSPECTION

An order to produce documents for inspection can be sought at any time in the proceedings but it is only in exceptional circumstances that such an order will be made before the Statement of Claim has been served (*Roper v Slack & Parr* [1981] CLY 2165).

A party wishing to inspect the documents of another party should serve a notice to produce the documents for inspection using Form 11 (Appendix C) of the Rules.

The recipient of such a Form 11 notice must reply within either two or four days of receipt using a Form 12 (Appendix C) notice, depending on whether all or only some of the documents referred to have been set forth in an affidavit or list of documents. In his reply he must state a time within three days, at which the documents may be inspected at his solicitors office. In the case of bankers books or other books of account or books in constant use in trade or business, inspection may take place at their usual place of custody i.e. bank, office premises. If objection is made to allowing inspection of any document, the grounds of objection must be stated in the Form 12 notice (O.31, r.17.).

Failure to allow inspection   If inspection of any document referred to in the pleadings or in any affidavit, is refused the party so refusing will not be permitted to use that document in evidence unless he can satisfy the Court that be has good and sufficient cause or excuse for refusing e.g. that the document relates solely to his own title, he being the defendant, or that it is subject to privilege. He is also liable, if a plaintiff, to have his proceedings struck out, or, if a defendant his defence may be struck out (O.31, r.21.)

Application to the Master for an order for inspection   An application before the Master for an order for inspection under O.31, r.18 (O.63, r.6) will only be necessary if (a) No reply is received to a Form 11 notice or (b) if the party served with a Form 11 notice omits to give such notice of a time for inspection or objects to giving inspection or offers inspection elsewhere than at the offices of his solicitor or if appropriate (see O.31, r.17) at their usual place of custody.

The Master may make an order for inspection in such place and in such manner as he may think fit.

Procedure   Motion on notice
2 clear days' notice
4 clear days for personal service

Proofs
        (a) Notice of motion
        (b) Grounding affidavit required in certain
             circumstances (O.31, r.18(1))
        (c) Affidavit of service of (a) and (b)
        (d) Copy pleadings, affidavits, Court Orders etc.

The grounding affidavit should state what documents the applicant wishes to inspect, his entitlement to inspection and his grounds for his belief that they are in the respondent's possession, power or control, except where the documents were referred to in the pleadings or affidavits of the party against whom the application is made, or disclosed in his affidavit or list of documents (O.31, r.18(1)).

Although there is no express provision in the Rules for inspection of premises or work processes, the High Court has made such an order under Order 50 r.4 and 5 (*Bula Ltd v Tara Mines* [1987] IR 85).

Bankers books   Order 63, r.1(17) states that the Master may make an Order under the Bankers Books Evidence Acts, 1879 and 1959. Under s. 7 of the Bankers Books Evidence Act, 1879 (the 'Principal Act'), as amended by the Bankers Books Evidence (Amendment) Act, 1959, any party to a legal proceeding may apply to a Court or judge for an order of inspection of a bankers book even though the bank in question is not a party to the proceedings. Section 9(2) of the Principal Act (as amended) defines 'bankers' books' as including any bank records used in the ordinary business of a bank, cover documents in manuscript, typed, printed or stencilled documents, documents which are created by any other mechanical or partly mechanical process and documents produced by any photographic or photostatic process. See *J.B. O'C. v P.C.D.* [1985] IR 265, as to what is included in the definition of books; and also *Larkins v N.U.M.* [1985] IR 671.

The expressions 'bank' and 'banker' are defined by s. 9 (as amended) to include named Banks, any other person who is the holder of a licence issued by the Central Bank, the Post Office savings bank and other named savings banks. It does not include the Central Bank.

The Master may make an order under s. 7 of the Principal Act granting the applicant liberty to inspect and take copies of any entries in a bankers' book. The inspection sought must be for the purpose of the legal proceedings.

The Master may make such an order *ex parte* on grounding affidavit, which should state the name of the accounts to be looked at,and without summoning the bank or any other party. The order must be served on the bank at least three clear days before the inspection is due to take place.

Copies may be ordered as an alternative O.31, r.20 allows the Master, instead of ordering inspection of the original books (whether bankers' books or business books), to order a copy of any entries made in those books to be furnished and verified by affidavit. The deponent must have examined and compared the copy with the original entries. The affidavit must state whether or not there are, in the original book, any erasures, interlineations or alterations and if so, must state exactly what they are. Should the Master make such an order,he is not thereby precluded from later ordering inspection of the book from which the copy was taken.

Costs of the application Section 8 of the Principal Act provides that the Court or Judge (including the Master) has a discretion as to the costs of the application. If the costs, or any part of them, were occasioned by any default or delay on the part of the bank, then the Master may order the bank to pay such costs to any party. Such an order for costs is enforceable as if the bank was a party to the proceedings.

Business books Where inspection of business books is sought, the Master similarly may order that copies be made of the relevant entries and verified by affidavit rather than grant an order for inspection under O.30, r.20. The procedure is the same as for bankers books (above). Under O.31, r.20 an application for an order for inspection must be grounded on affidavit, unless inspection is sought of documents referred to in the pleadings or affidavits of the party against whom the application is made or disclosed in his affidavit (of discovery) or list of documents from which the copy was made (O.31, r.20(1))

The right to inspect may be implied eg: in the terms of a commercial agreement. Such right must not be abused and inspection of confidential business documents must be carried out solely for the purpose of ascertaining the rights of the parties and in preparing for litigation or arbitration (see *'Winterthur' Swiss Insurance Co. v I.C.I.* [1989] ILRM 13).

Grounds of objection to inspection A party may object to producing documents for inspection on the following grounds. The list is not intended to be exhaustive.

(1) The documents are not in the possession, power or control of the respondent party. If such objection is raised an application should be made by way of motion on notice grounded or affidavit under O.30, r.20(3).

(2) An order for inspection is not necessary either for disposing fairly of the cause or matter, or for saving costs (O.31, r.18(2))

(3) An agreement exists between the parties as to non disclosure. An applicant may overcome this objection by showing inspection is necessary to fairly dispose of the cause or matter.

(4) That producing the documents for inspection would lead to self incrimination or possible penalty.

(5) The documents are in a foreign country. Where inspection was sought under the Bankers Books Evidence Acts, 1879 and 1959,

of books of account held at the New York branch of a bank incorporated in this jurisdiction, the High Court held that it had no power under the Acts to order inspection of the books in a foreign country: see *Chemical Bank v McCormack* [1983] ILRM 350 *per* Carroll J.

(6) Privilege (see *Silver Hill Duckling Ltd v Minister for Agriculture* [1987] IR 289). A claim to privilege should be made on affidavit with the nature of the claim clearly stated. Such a claim is usually made in an affidavit of Discovery. The Master or the High Court (where a claim is disputed) may require sight of the documents in order to determine the validity of the claim (O.31, r.20(2.)). The inquiry will focus on the dominant purpose for which the document was made or drafted. Once a privileged document has passed into the hands of another party then, prima facie the privilege has been lost unless it was also a confidential document (see *Webster v James Chapman & Co.* [1989] 3 All ER 939).

Classes of privilege The following are the main categories of privilege. The list is not exhaustive as it is clear from the authorities that the categories of privilege are not closed:

1. Professional privilege Documents prepared with a view to securing legal assistance other than advice are not privileged (see *Smurfit Puribas Bank Ltd v A.A.B. Export Finance Ltd* [1990] IR 469) A document is privileged if drafted for the purpose of obtaining legal advice and not merely clarification of instructions (see *P.J. Carrigan Ltd v Norwich Union Fire Society Ltd* [1987] IR 618; *Silver Hill Duckling v Minister for Agriculture, supra*).

Dishonest conduct will preclude the protection normally afforded by professional privilege: see *Murphy v Kirwin* (unreported, High Court, Costello J, 9 April 1992).

2. Statutory privilege An example may be found in s. 31 of the

Central Bank Act 1942 (see *Cully v Northern Bank Finance Corporation Ltd* [1984] ILRM 683).

3. State privilege   When such a claim is made the Master or the High Court must determine whether any potential injustice which would ensue from a refusal to grant inspection would be greater than the damage to the public interest which might result from granting the order to produce the documents for inspection (see *Geraghty v Minister for Local Government* [1975] IR 300; *Folens & Co. Ltd v Minister for Education* [1981] ILRM 21; *Ahern v Minister for Industry & Commerce* [1990] IR 55).

4. Public interest privilege   Examples of documents to which such privilege might attach are police reports and probation service records in wardship proceedings. In addition details of interviews may be privileged:

(a) Priest and penitent: see *Cook v Carroll* [1945] IR 515.

(b) Journalists: see *In re Kevin O'Kelly* (1974) 108 ILTR 97 where the Court of Criminal Appeal held that a journalist was not any more constitutionally or legally immune than any other citizen from being required to disclose information received in confidence. The fact that a communication was made under terms of expressed or implied confidence does not of itself create a privilege against disclosure. So far as the administration of justice is concerned the public has a right to every man's evidence, except for those protected by a constitutional or other established and recognized privilege (*per* Walsh J).

INTERROGATORIES

The origin of interrogatories lies in a form of discovery known as discovery of facts, whereby a person could be directed to answer as to the existence of facts within his knowledge and relevant to the dispute. Each party is entitled to a knowledge of the material facts on which the other relies to support his case (see *Eade v Jacobs*, Ex D 335).

An order for delivery of interrogatories   O.63, r.1(6) provides that
the Master may make an order for delivery of interrogatories. In
actions where relief is sought on the ground of fraud or breach of trust,
a plaintiff or defendant may deliver interrogatories in writing for the
examination of the other parties without any order for that purpose.

In all other cases the leave of the Court must be sought (O.31, r.1)
A plaintiff cannot deliver interrogatories before delivering his statement of claim. A defendant must file his defence before delivering
interrogatories (O.31, r.1)

The order may be made against a third party   The procedure was
traditionally only available against parties to the action. However,
O.31, r.29 now provides that on the application of any party to the
action, a third party may by leave of the Court, be directed to answer
such interrogatories if he is likely to be in a position to give evidence
relevant to any issue. The provisions of O. 31 will apply *mutatis
mutandis* as if the order had been made inter partes.

An applicant party under r. 29 must indemnify the third party in
respect of his costs reasonably incurred.

Reason for interrogatories   The purpose of interrogatories is to
clarify and narrow the issues between the parties through admissions
made in response to the interrogatories, thus obtaining evidence which
might otherwise be unavailable. A copy of the interrogatories which
the applicant wishes to deliver must be delivered with the notice of
application for leave to deliver them (unless otherwise ordered) and a
copy must be made available to the Court for consideration (O.31, r.2).
An order granting leave to deliver interrogatories is not general in its
form but specifically relates to the interrogatories delivered with the
notice of application and considered by the Court.

Whether interrogatories should be ordered   When considering such an application, the Court is obliged by the Rules to take into account any offer made by the party sought to be interrogated, to deliver particulars, make admissions or produce documents relating to any matter in question. The correct test to be applied, is whether the interrogatories are necessary for the purpose of disposing fairly of the cause or matter or for saving costs: see *Quilligan v Sugrue* (unreported, High Court, Hamilton J, 13 February 1984) (O.31, r.2).

The Master's Order   The Master may make an order for deliver of interrogatories upon such terms as to security for costs or otherwise as he thinks fit.

Type and form of interrogatories   Interrogatories must relate to the matters in question in the action. They need not be shown to be conclusive on the questions in issue, it being sufficient that they have some bearing on the question and that they might form a step in establishing liability. It is not necessary to show that a question is in respect of something which the applicant does not already know (see *J. & L.S. Goodbody Ltd v The Clyde Shipping Co. Ltd* unreported, Supreme Court, 9 May 1967.) They must be drafted in such a manner as to require a 'yes' or 'no' answer and should be set out as in Form 8 (Appendix C) of the Rules.

Where interrogatories are delivered to two or more opposite parties they are bad on their face if when delivered, they do not have a footnote stating which questions each party is required to answer (see *McClatchey v Reilly & Ulster Bank Ltd* [1960] NI 118). Rule 5 governs the situation where the respondent party is a body corporate.

Reply to interrogatories   Interrogatories must be answered by affidavit within ten days of delivery or such further time as has been allowed by the Court O.31, r.8. The affidavit should be as Form 9 (Appendix C) of the Rules.

Time for delivery of interrogatories Interrogatories will not be struck out merely on the ground that the application for leave to deliver was not made before the matter was set down for trial (*McClatchey v Reilly & Ulster Bank Ltd* [1960] NI 118). Order 31, r. 24 deals with the way in which use may be made of answers to interrogatories at the trial of the action.

Procedure   Motion on notice
       2 clear days
       4 clear days for personal service

Proofs   (a) Notice of motion
       (b) Interrogatories
       (c) Affidavit of service
       (d) Copy pleadings, Court orders and affidavits
         to date.

Grounds of objection to interrogatories The Rules (O.31, r.6) list certain grounds of objection but the list is not intended to be exhaustive. Any objection to answering a particular interrogatory should be stated in the affidavit in answer. The grounds include:

(a) the interrogatories are scandalous

(b) the interrogatories are irrelevant

(c) the interrogatories are not *bona fide* for the purpose of the cause or matter

(d) the matters inquired into are not sufficiently material at this stage

(e) the interrogatories are not intended to be exhaustive

(f) the interrogatories are unnecessary either for disposing fairly of the cause or matter or for saving costs.

(g) the interrogatories are premature

(h) the applicant is seeking to gather evidence to substantiate or formulate his claim (ie. 'a fishing expedition'). The interrogatories relate solely to the evidence of the party to be interrogated.

(i) the form of the interrogatories is incorrect. The Master has discretion in amending the form of the interrogatories and will do so to clarify the question asked and so as to require a 'yes' or 'no' answer.

(j) Privilege. If a respondent is claiming privilege he must do so on oath in a similar manner to such a claim in an affidavit of discovery. The nature of the privilege being claimed must be clearly stated.

In addition, a party to whom interrogatories are delivered, may apply to the High Court, by way of motion on notice, within seven days of the service to have them struck out on the grounds that they are prolix, oppressive, unnecessary or scandalous (O.31, r.1)

Failure to comply If the respondent fails to answer the interrogatories on affidavit (Form 9 Appendix C of the Rules) within the time allowed or gives an insufficient answer, application may be made to the High Court by way of motion on notice, requiring the respondent to answer, or to answer further, either by affidavit or by *viva voce* examination O.31, r.11. Rule 10 provides that the sufficiency or otherwise of any such replying affidavit shall be determined by the Court on motion and no exception shall be taken to such affidavit. A continued failure or refusal to answer, may result in the respondent's proceedings or his defence (as appropriate) being struck out and in extreme cases may render the party in default or his solicitor, liable to attachment (O.31, rr.21-23).

4

Recognition and Enforcement of Foreign Judgments

The Jurisdiction of Courts and Enforcement of Judgments (European Communities) Act, 1988, came into effect on 1 June 1988 (SI No. 91 of 1988). The Act was designed to meet Ireland's obligations under the 1968 Brussels Convention on the jurisdiction and enforcement of judgments in civil and commercial matters, the 1971 Protocol on interpretation and the 1978 Accession conventions. The Jurisdiction of Courts and Enforcement of Judgments Act, 1993 came into effect on 1 December 1993 and permits ratification of two related conventions the 1989 Accession Convention which enabled Spain and Portugal to accede to the 1968 Brussels Convention and the Lugano Convention on jurisdiction and the enforcement of judgments in civil and commercial matters.

The 1988 Act led to changes in the rules of the Superior, Circuit and District courts. This chapter deals only with the jurisdiction of the Master under s. 5 of the Act. The relevant rules are contained in O. 42A of the Rules. The order governs protective measures and the enforcement of judgments under the Act of 1988. The contracting states now the parties to the Convention include Germany, France, Italy, Luxembourg, Netherlands (including Aruba), Ireland, Belgium, Denmark, the U.K. and Greece.

Under s. 5 of the Act all applications for the recognition and enforcement of a foreign judgment within this State, shall be made to the Master of the High Court and shall be determined by him by order (including an order for the recognition or enforcement of a judgment in part only) in accordance with the Conventions and the 1971 Protocol.

The Act also covers the recognition and enforcement of authentic instruments and Court settlements. These are civil law concepts and such applications are dealt with (*ex parte*) by the High Court at first instance and not by the Master who deals with judgments only.

The term 'judgment' is defined with reference to Article 25 of the 1968 Convention, and includes any judgment (including a consent order) given by a Court or Tribunal of a contracting State. The Convention deals only with 'civil and commercial matters' and does not extend to revenue, customs or administrative matters. It does *not* apply to the following:

1. Judgments concerning the status or legal capacity of natural persons.

2. Judgments concerning rights in property arising out of a matrimonial relationship (see Family Law, pp. 54f *post*).

3. Judgments concerning wills and succession.

4. Bankruptcy of winding up proceedings, judicial arrangements, compositions and analogous proceedings.

5. Social security matters.

6. Arbitration.

The 1993 Act provides for a new jurisdiction in respect of employment contracts.

In the case of *L.T.U. v Eurocontrol* [1976] ECR 1541, [1977] 1 CMLR 88, it was held that the phrase 'civil and commercial matters' is to be construed by having regard, not to the national law of the contracting state, but to the aims and system of the Convention and to the general principles of E.C. and international law.

A party seeking to enforce a judgment in a Convention case, is obliged to use the Convention procedure even if other more expedient procedures are available. See *De Wolf* [1976] ECR 1759.

Once it has been established that the judgment is one to which the

Convention applies, an application may be made, *ex parte*, before the Master of the High Court for the recognition and enforcement of such judgment and for such protective measures as are necessary to ensure its enforcement. Such application must be grounded on affidavit (see Practice and procedure *post*)

Article 34, which contains transitional provisions states that the Conventions and protocol shall only apply to legal proceedings instituted after the entry into force of the Conventions in both the State of origin and the State in which recognition or enforcement of the foreign judgment is sought.

The fact that the conventions came into force on different dates in the various contracting States can lead to difficulties, as the following hypothetical example will ellucidate. Proceedings were issued in England in November 1987 and judgment was given there in August 1988. The date on which the provisions of the Convention came into effect in the U.K. was 1 January 1987 and in Ireland, 1 June 1988.

The judgment will be recognised and enforced in Ireland only if:

1. The proceedings were instituted and judgment was given in the U.K. after 1 June 1988, *or*

2. If the judgment was given after 1 June 1988, but the proceedings were instituted *before* that date, where the U.K. Court or tribunal's jurisdiction was founded on principles which accord with the Convention's provisions on jurisdiction.[1] The above example falls into the second category.

Recognition and enforcement will *not* be granted if the foreign judgment was given *before* 1 June 1988.[2]

PRACTICE AND PROCEDURE

Order 42A governs the practice and procedure for all applications under s. 5 of the Convention. Order 42A, r.5 requires that such

---

1. See Article 34 of the Convention.   2. See s. 5 of the 1988 Act.

applications be grounded on affidavit specifying the protective measures (if any) requested by the applicant. The affidavit must exhibit the following:

1. *A copy of the judgment* to be enforced, duly certified or authenticated by the authorities of the state in question.

2. In the case of a default judgment, *documentary evidence* (original or certified true copies) going towards establishing that the party in default was served with the proceedings in sufficient time to allow him to prepare his defence e.g. duly indorsed writ (U.K.), affidavit of service duly sworn.

3. *Documents which*, according to the national laws of the contracting State where judgment was given, *establish that the judgment is enforceable* and has been served on the defendant. A certificate equivalent to that provided for by s.12 of the Act of 1988 should be included. Note: Documents must be provided showing service of both the originating process and of the judgment.

4. *Legal aid documents*. If the applicant is in receipt of legal aid in the state in which judgment was given, Article 44 provides for such applicant to be legally aided in making his application for the enforcement of that judgment. This entitlement only covers the initial *ex parte* application and is governed by national laws.

If the necessary documentation is not produced, the Master may allow time for their production and adjourn the application,[3] or he may dispense with the requirements. A translation of any documents in a foreign language should be provided, certified by the authorities of the state where the judgment was given.

The grounding affidavit   The following information must be contained in the affidavit grounding the application for recognition and enforcement of a foreign judgment:

3.   See Article 48.

1. Whether the said judgment provides for the payment of a sum of money.

2. Whether, according to the law of the State in which judgment was given, interest is recoverable and if so details of the rate of interest and the dates between which interest is being claimed.

3. The applicant for enforcement must give an address for service of proceedings upon him within the jurisdiction area of the enforcement court[4] or as the case may be should apply for the appointment of a guardian *ad litem*, upon whom proceedings may be served, providing the Master with the necessary details.

Once the applicant has satisfied the Master that the documentation is in order and the necessary information has been supplied to the Court, the Master may only refuse the application in the following circumstances:

1. Where it would be contrary to public policy to grant enforcement of the judgment e.g. where there is evidence that the judgment was obtained by fraud or otherwise than in accordance with the national laws of the state in which it was obtained. The public policy referred to is the public policy of the state in which enforcement is being sought.

2. If the recognition and enforcement of the foreign judgment would breach the rules of natural justice, then the Master may refuse to make the order sought. The most obvious example under this heading is where a default judgment has been granted in circumstances where the defendant was not duly served or was otherwise not given adequate notice of the proceedings. The law governing the curing of defective service is that of the judgment rendering state. In *Isabelle Lancray SA v Peters and Sickert KG* [1990] 1 ECR 2725 the Court of Justice held that even where the foreign proceedings were served in sufficient time to arrange for a

4. See Article 33.

defence, the subsequent default judgment will still not be recognised if the service was defective. This was reiterated in *Minalmet GmbH v Brandeis Ltd* [1992] 1 ECR 5661

3. Where the judgment is irreconcilable with a judgment given in a dispute between the same parties in the state in which enforcement is being sought.

The Master will not enter into any consideration of the substance of the judgment.[5] An applicant seeking recognition and enforcement of a foreign judgment may also seek protective measures pending an appeal e.g. measures to ensure the maintenance of sufficient assets within the jurisdiction to meet the judgment.

The Master should be given notice of such an application and if so, the Master has no discretion and must grant the protective measures sought. In *Elwyn Cottons v Pearle Designs* [1989] IR 9 the High Court reviewed a decision of the Master where he refused an application made by the plaintiff for protective measures. The Master had granted the plaintiff's application for the recognition and enforcement of a judgment of the English High Court, but then refused a further application for a Mareva-type injunction.

Under Article 39 of the Convention, protective measures may be sought within one month of the perfection of the Masters enforcement order and s. 11(3) of the Act of 1988 provides that the Master *shall* include a provision granting any of the protective measures applied for as part of his enforcement order. Carroll J held that s. 11 does not vest discretion in the Master with regard to protective measures. The Master must grant the measure sought provided the Irish High Court would have jurisdiction to grant that measure in respect of an Irish judgment. It was held that once the Master had made an enforcement order it was unnecessary for the plaintiff to make a separate application to another judicial authority seeking protective measures pending an appeal (*Cappelloni & Aqualini v Pelkinans* [1985] ECR 3147 followed).

5. See Articles 29 and 34.

The appropriate form of an order for the recognition and enforcement of a foreign judgment made by the Master under s. 5 was considered by Blayney J and by the Supreme Court on appeal in the case of *Rhatigan v Textiles y Confecciones* [1989] IR 19; [1990] IR 126. On the defendant's application, the Master had made an order under the Act of 1988 for the recognition and enforcement of four English judgments against the plaintiff who then challenged the validity of the Master's order. The matter came before Blayney J by way of special case. The court was requested to determine two issues,

(1) Whether the Master's order was a nullity and *ultra vires* the provisions of the Act of 1988 on the grounds that it contained no address on its face for service of process within the jurisdiction nor did it disclose that the judgments to be enforced were judgments of a contracting state and

(2) Whether the Master was entitled to authorise enforcement of the judgments as judgments to which the Convention applied.

The High Court, Blayney J, held that Article 33 of the Convention required that the applicants address for service of process within the jurisdiction be supplied to the Master at the time of the application and as part of it. It is not essential that the address be included in the order itself. Nor is it necessary to specify the contracting state in which judgment was obtained in a contested case such as this, as clearly the respondent in such a case knows the country in question.

On the second question the High Court, Blayney J, found that on the evidence before him the Master was entitled to conclude that the judgments were enforceable under the Convention as all four sets of proceedings had been instituted after the Convention had come into force in the U.K. On appeal to the Supreme Court the findings of the High Court were upheld. Griffin J in delivering judgment stated that apart from requiring that the application must give an address for service of the process within the jurisdiction and that the document referred to in Articles 46 and 47 shall be attached to the application, these being requirements of European community law, all the procedures including the necessary proofs to be adduced are governed by national law.

APPEALS

An appeal may be taken to the High Court against a refusal by the Master to grant an order under s. 5 of the Act of 1988 for the recognition and enforcement of a foreign judgment. Such an appeal must be lodged within five weeks of the date of perfection of the Masters order and proceeds by way of Motion on Notice (see *Firma P v Firma K* [1984] ECR 3033).

An appeal may also be made by the defendant against an order of the Master granting enforcement, see Chapter 1. The grounds of appeal are strictly limited by the Convention itself (see articles 27 and 28) and must not involve the Court in a review of the substance of the judgment (see Articles 29-34 and *Westpac Banking Corporation v Dempsey*, unreported, High Court, Morris J, 19 November 1992).

FAMILY LAW AND THE CONVENTION

In accordance with Article 1.1 the Convention does not apply to 'the status or legal capacity of natural persons, rights in property arising out of a matrimonial relationship, wills and succession'.

In *DeCavel v DeCavel (No. 1)* [1979] ECR 1055; [1979] 2 CMR 547, the Court interpreted the exclusion of 'rights in property arising out of a matrimonial relationship' by the Brussels Convention on Jurisdiction 1968, in the context of an interlocutory freezing of the assets of a divorcing couple by the French Court considering the divorce petition, the assets being located in Germany, to the effect that its enforcement in Germany is not covered by the Convention unless the assets have no connection with the marriage.

However, the Convention may be used to enforce the payment of maintenance which it is intended to provide for the support of a spouse or child. Section 7 of the Act of 1988 provides for the enforcement of

a maintenance order made within one of the other contracting states.
An application may be made to the Master of the High Court *ex parte*
for enforcement of the order, in accordance with O. 42A, r.5. Rule 6
sets out the contents of the grounding affidavit, as before. Where the
Master refuses the application, the applicant has five weeks from the
date of perfection of the order in which to appeal to the High Court
(O. 42A, r.12). In addition pursuant to s. 6(2) of the Act of 1988 arrears
of maintenance which had accumulated prior to the issue of an enforcement order may be declared by the Master of the High Court, on
the application of the maintenance creditor, to be enforceable, and
shall be of the same force and effect as if it were a judgment of the
High Court and proceedings for its enforcement may be taken accord-
ingly. Section 6 also applies to the situation were a lump sum maintenance judgment is given in another contracting state.

A Listing and Summary of the Rules

which apply to the Master's Court

In this chapter the following abbreviations are used: 'EP' = *ex parte*; 'N' = on notice (the notice period for motions is two clear days if served on the respondent's solicitor, or four clear days for personal service); 'A' = affidavit of service; 'C' = copy pleadings; 'G' = grounding affidavit; 'R' = reference to the Master.

O.12, r.8   APPEARANCE—fictitious or illusory address stated in the memorandum. The plaintiff may bring a motion before the Master to have the Appearance set aside

EP.A (of summons) .G.

O.13   JUDGMENT IN DEFAULT OF APPEARANCE—O.12 states that a defendant to a special summons may enter an appearance at any time before judgment except in actions for the recovery of land (leave of the Court necessary O.12, r.15) but he will not be heard unless he first enters an appearance

rr.1-16   An appearance must be entered within 8 days of service of a plenary or summary summons (exclusive of the day of

O.12, r.2   service) unless the Court orders otherwise. In some actions where an appearance has not been entered within the time allowed, the plaintiff may enter judgment in the Central Office by filing an affidavit of service of the originating summons and where appropriate, a statement of claim (see chapter 2(b) for further details).

In the following cases under O. 13, a preliminary application must be made to the Master before judgment will be entered in the Central office. In addition, in any matter coming before the Master under O.13, r.1-15, the Master may, in lieu of granting liberty to enter final judgment, place the summons in the Court list (O.13, r.16).

O.13, r.1   INFANT OR PERSON OF UNSOUND MIND NOT SO FOUND—If the defendant falls into either category, a preliminary application must be made for the appointment of a guardian ad litem upon whom the proceedings must be served. The summons and notice of motion must be served on the father/ guardian/custodian assigned by the Master. Liberty to enter final judgment may be granted by the Master if such guardian fails to appear.

> N (six days for notice of motion). A.C.
> There are strict service requirements
> under O.13, r.1 which must be observed.

O.13   MONEYLENDING—Where an originating summons is indorsed with a claim for a liquidated demand, judgment in default of appearance may be entered in the Central office by filing an affidavit of debt (O.13, r.18) an affidavit of service (O.13, r.2) except where the claim arises from a moneylending or hire purchase agreement, when leave to enter final judgment must first be sought from the Master.

r. 3-4   APPLICATION FOR LIBERTY TO ENTER FINAL JUDGMENT IN DEFAULT OF APPEARANCE—The notice of motion will not be issued until the time limit for entering an appearance has expired and a proper affidavit of service of the summons has been filed (see O.13, r.14.2 for notice and service requirement); s. 1 of the Moneylenders Act 1900, as amended by s. 17 of the Moneylenders (Amendment) Act 1933 applies. When dealing with such an application, the Master may exercise all the powers of the 'Court' under the Moneylenders Acts to,

— re-open the transaction in question if the interest, charges or premiums claimed appear excessive. If the interest rate charged exceeds 39% per annum it is automatically presumed to be excessive (s. 17 of the Act of 1933).

— require the moneylender to produce his moneylenders certificate and require such particulars as the Master considers desirable to be indorsed on the certificate (s. 17(2) of the Act of 1933).

— after considering all the circumstances, set aside either wholly or in part, revise or alter any security given or agreement made in respect of money lent by the moneylender and if the moneylender has parted with the security, may order him to indemnify the borrower or other person sued (s. 17(2) of the Act of 1933).

— give leave to enter final judgment for the whole or any part of the claim and give such directions as to service as he deems just.

— in lieu of giving or refusing to grant leave to enter final judgment, place the matter in the Court list for O.13, r.16 hearing.

Once liberty to enter final judgment has been granted by the Master, judgment may be entered in the Central office by filing an affidavit of debt.   N.A.C.G.

HIRE PURCHASE AND CREDIT SALE AGREEMENTS—An application for liberty to enter final judgment in default of appearance must be made before the Master in the same manner as applies to moneylending agreements.

If the Master is not satisfied that the requirements of the regulatory legislation have been met or if the defendant appears and there is a clear dispute between the parties, the Master may place the summons in the Court list for hearing (O.13, r.16).

Once leave to enter final judgment has been granted by the Master, an affidavit in the form prescribed by O.13, r.16 must be filed in the Central Office before judgment can be entered. The affidavit must contain averments that ss. 3 and 4 of the Hire Purchase Act 1946 as amended by the Hire Purchase (Amendment) Act 1960, have been complied with. The sections set out the *minimum* statutory requirements relating to such agreements.

N.A.C.G.

Notice and service requirements are the same as for money-lending agreements.

Not less than four clear days notice must be given of an application under O.13, r.3.

O.13, r.4-5 RECOVERY OF LAND—In an action for recovery of land commenced by *summary summons* where no appearance has been entered, or an appearance has been entered but the defence is limited to part of the land or to an undivided share of the land only, the plaintiff may either:

(i) Enter judgment in the Central Office under O.13, r.4 for recovery of possession of the land or such part of it as the defence does not cover. Such judgment will be for recovery of possession only. The plaintiff must proceed by action for the remainder of his claim whether for mesne profits, rent, damages and/or costs. If the claim for recovery of land is based on non- payment of rent, then no judgment will be entered until the landlord or his agent, receiver or clerk has filed an affidavit containing an averment that at least one year's rent was due, over and above all just and fair allowances at the date the proceedings were commenced. (note O.37, r.15).

(ii) Set the entire claim down for hearing on such day as

the Master shall fix. On the hearing of the summary summons the Master may give such judgment as he considers the plaintiff to be entitled to.

O.A.C.G.

O.13, r.6
O.63, r.2
The Master does not have jurisdiction to hear actions for recovery of land commenced by plenary summons, save that where the High Court has granted judgment in default of appearance to a plenary summons, the Court may refer the ascertainment of any damages to which the plaintiff is entitled to the Master.

O.13, r.13
LIBERTY TO ENTER JUDGMENT FOR COSTS ONLY—In any case where the plaintiff is not entitled to enter judgment in the Central Office in default of appearance and where the plaintiff finds it unnecessary to proceed with his claim, he may nevertheless seek to recover his costs. Judgment for costs may only be entered by leave of the Master obtained by way of motion on notice. The notice of motion must be filed and served in the same manner as the originating summons or in such other manner as the Master may direct.

N.A.C.G.

O.13, r.19
The Master does not have jurisdiction to entertain a claim for interest under s.22 of the Courts Act, 1981. If a plaintiff seeks interest he may apply *ex parte* to the High Court for an order for judgment inclusive of such interest under O.13, r.19. A grounding affidavit is necessary.

O.13, r.17
SUMMARY SUMMONS INDORSED WITH A CLAIM FOR ACCOUNT OR INVOLVING THE TAKING OF AN ACCOUNT— Where the defendant fails to enter an appearance in such cases, the Master shall forthwith make an order for the proper accounts with all necessary inquiries and directions

before judgment in default can be entered in the Central
Office.

N.A.C.G.

O.13, r.17
O.37, r.13

SUMMARY SUMMONS INDORSED WITH A CLAIM FOR AN
ACCOUNT OR INVOLVING THE TAKING OF AN ACCOUNT—If
a defendant fails to enter an appearance in such cases the
Master will make an order forthwith for the proper accounts
with all necessary inquiries and directions before judgment
can be entered in the Central Office.

N.A.C.G.

O. 29,
rr. 6-7

SECURITY FOR COSTS—The High Court hears the sub-
stantive application, which proceeds by way of motion on
notice, grounded on affidavit. If the High Court grants such
order, it will then refer the matter to the Master. The Master
will determine the amount of such security, the time,
manner and form of its payment and to whom such security
must be given.

The ordinary practice is to order an amount for security
for costs of not more than about one third of the costs which
would probably be incurred by the defendants. The principles were laid down in *Thalle v Soares* [1957] IR 182,
and applied in *Fallon v An Bord Pleanala* [1991] ILRM
799. However, in an application for security pursuant to the
Companies Act 1963 'sufficient' security must be given—
Thalle v Soares supra, and there is no rule requiring the
deduction of 2/3 from the assessed amount of costs. see also
Probets v Glackin & Ors (unreported, *ex tempore*, High
Court, Keane J, 23 November 1992).

N.A.G.

O.29, r.7

SECURITY BY BOND—Where a bond is given as security for
costs then unless the Master otherwise orders, such bond is

given to the applicant. In any matrimonial cause or matter the bond shall be given to the Master.

O.30   SIDE BAR ORDERS—*post*.

O.31   DISCOVERY, INSPECTION AND INTERROGATORIES (see chapter 3).

O.36, r.4   MOTION FOR DIRECTIONS—In all Probate or Admiralty actions commenced by plenary summons and in Matrimonial Proceedings commenced by Petition (see O.70, r.1), the plaintiff must bring a motion for Directions before the Master within 14 days after the pleadings have closed. The Master determines the issues to be decided at the trial of the action (Counsel may have these drafted and handed in to the Master who may approve them or may alter them) and in addition will fix the mode of trial (judge and jury or judge alone), and make any ancillary order which he deems necessary or expedient. If the plaintiff fails to apply for Directions within the time limit specified, the defendant may make the application after 14 days default (i.e. 28 days after the pleadings have closed)

Following the Master's directions, the plaintiff should set the action down for hearing.

N.C.

Note: In nullity proceedings the citation must have been indorsed in accordance with O.70 r.11 (Form 3 App L) and filed and either an appearance entered or an affidavit of service of the citation filed (O.70 r.14—Form 4 App L) before the petitioner may proceed with a motion for directions (see further O.70).

O.36, r.8 DISPUTE INVOLVING MATTERS OF ACCOUNT—If at any time after proceedings have been issued, it appears that the matters in dispute consist wholly or partly of matters of account which cannot be conveniently tried in the ordinary way, then the High Court may, on the application of either party, refer the matters of account to the Master on such terms as it shall think reasonable.

O.36,
rr.43-49
O.63, r.2 REFERENCE TO THE MASTER AS TO DAMAGES—Order 36 governs the trial of actions or proceedings. Where the High Court is faced with an assessment of the damages to which a party is entitled and the amount is substantially a matter of calculation, then the Court may direct that the amount for which final judgment is to be entered shall be ascertained by the Master following an inquiry. Under O.63, r.2 the Master may in any proceedings assess any damages to which a party is entitled on consent of all parties concerned.

O.36, r.43 The Master has complete discretion in the arrangement and regulation of his inquiry and has like powers to the
O.36, r.44 High Court in his assessment of damages including the power to *subpoena* witnesses or documents.

O.36, r.44 The Master will take down and preserve the evidence presented at the time of his inquiry (see O.123, r.2).

O.36, r.45 Following his inquiry the Master will issue a certificate in which the result will be stated. The certificate will stand confirmed unless challenged within four days of filing by way of a motion on notice to set aside or vary the certificate. The motion is brought before the High Court and the notice
O.36, r.46 must specify the grounds on which it is intended to apply to set aside or vary the Master's certificate.

Following confirmation of such certificate, final judgment may be entered in the Central Office for the certified amount.

O.39, r.42   CERTIFICATE OF DEPOSITION—COMMISSION ROGATOIRE
—A commission rogatoire is a letter of request from a
foreign Court or Tribunal asking that the testimony of a

O.39, r.39   witness living in this jurisdiction be taken by a Commissioner appointed by the High Court for that purpose.

Once the Commissioner has taken the evidence, he must forward it to the Master. The Master will attach to it, a certificate in the form stated in the Rules (see Form 2, App. D, Part III). The deposition, the certificate and commission rogatoire are then returned to the Minister for foreign affairs for transmission to the foreign Court or Tribunal or

O.39, r.42   they may be sent directly by the Master to the Consul or other diplomatic representative of the country in question.

O.42A   THE ENFORCEMENT OF FOREIGN JUDGMENTS (see chapter 4).

O.43, r.3   SEQUESTRATION—Motion for Directions.

Before an Order for sequestration can be issued, the person so entitled must apply to the Master for an order approving the sequestrator and obtaining directions as to his security and accounting. The Master may issue a certificate which must be filed in the Central Office. The order for sequestration may then issue directed to the approved

O.43, r.2   sequestrator.

N.G (exhibit Court Order or judgment)

O.50, r.15   COMPOUNDING A PENAL ACTION (i.e. a settlement or agreement among creditors, one of whom is the State, to settle the action for a certain sum).

Once the High Court has given leave to compound such action, the amount owing to the State must be paid in to the Master who will dispose of it for the benefit of the Exchequer.

<table>
<tr><td>O.63
O.63

r.1.1</td><td>SIDE BAR ORDERS—This Order deals most extensively with the Master and his jurisdiction.

The Master may make any such order except those listed at O.30, rr.17 and 18 which govern the renunciation of rights to Probate and Administration by failing to appear or to extract (see O.30 for a full list of side bar orders).</td></tr>
<tr><td>O.63,
r.1(2)</td><td>ANY ORDER WHICH MAY BE MADE AS A MATTER OF COURSE—This type of order is one made on an *ex parte* application and is an order to which a party is entitled to as of right. Such orders would deal with non-contentious matters.

EP.</td></tr>
<tr><td>O.63,
r.1(3)</td><td>AN ORDER FOR THE APPOINTMENT OF A GUARDIAN AD LITEM OF AN INFANT OR PERSON OF UNSOUND MIND NOT SO FOUND—When a guardian *ad litem* is being replaced an application is made under this rule. No order is required in the first instance where an infant's guardian *ad litem* enters an appearance (see O. 15, rr.16-21).

EP (note O.13, r.1)</td></tr>
<tr><td>O.63
r.1(4)</td><td>AN ORDER FOR A STATEMENT OF THE NAMES OF CO-PARTNERS IN ANY FIRM SUING OR BEING SUED

EP.</td></tr>
<tr><td>O.63
r.1(5)</td><td>ORDER FOR AN ENLARGEMENT OF TIME AS WHERE A PARTY HAS RUN OUT OF TIME FOR THE DOING OF ANY ACT OR TAKING ANY STEP UNDER THE RULES—The Master may *inter alia* make an order extending the time in which to lodge an appeal from the Circuit Court to the High Court—see *Éire Continental Trading Company v Clonmel Foods Ltd* [1955] IR 170, extending the time to deliver a statement</td></tr>
</table>

of claim, or for renewing a writ within twelve months of issue (see O.8).

N.A.G.

O.63, r.1(6)

DISCOVERY, INSPECTION & INTERROGATORIES (see chapter 3).

O.63, r.1(7)

ORDER FOR THE APPOINTMENT OR DISCHARGE OF A RECEIVER IN UNCONTESTED APPLICATIONS ONLY—See also O.63, r.1(24), O. 45, r. 9 and O. 50, rr. 5, 6 and 16.

N.A.G.C.

O.63, r.1(8)

ORDER DISMISSING AN ACTION WITH COSTS FOR WANT OF PROSECUTION OR FOR FAILURE TO MAKE AN AFFIDAVIT OF DISCOVERY OR TO ANSWER INTERROGATORIES (see chapter 3).

N.A.G.C.

O.63, r.1(9)

ORDER STRIKING OUT A DEFENCE WITH COSTS FOR FAILURE TO MAKE AN AFFIDAVIT OF DISCOVERY OR TO ANSWER INTERROGATORIES (see chapter 3).

N.A.G.C.

O.63, r.1(10)

ORDER FOR THE TAKING OF EVIDENCE ON COMMISSION—The order sets out the names of the parties to be examined, of the Commissioner and gives directions as to date, time and place. Usually the order will be made where the witness has gone abroad, or where the witness would be unable to attend the hearing of the action because of some infirmity. The Master must be satisfied that the application is made *bona fide*, that the evidence to be obtained is necessary for the proper determination of the issues between the parties (*McSweeney v Kavanagh* unreported, High Court, Hamilton J, 5 March 1984), that there is a good reason for the taking of evidence on commission, and that it will be effectual. See also O.39, r.4. Unless a request is made for the appointment of a particular individual as commissioner, then in practice the Master will appoint the most junior member of the Bar then present in Court.

N.A.C.

O.63,
r.1(11)

ORDER FOR DIRECTIONS AS TO SERVICE OF AN ORIGINATING SUMMONS NOT INTER PARTES OR AS TO OTHER PROCEDURE

E.P.

O.63,
r.1(12)

ORDER FOR THE ADDITION OR SUBSTITUTION OF A PARTY IN ANY ACTION OR PROCEEDING—This application may be made by either a plaintiff or a defendant, and must be grounded on affidavit.

N.A.C.G.

O.63,
r.1(13)

ORDER GRANTING THE APPLICANT LIBERTY TO INTERVENE AND APPEAR—See O.12, rr.14, 20 and O.64, r.14.

N. (to all parties). A.C.

O.63,
r.1(14)

CONSENT ORDER FOR THE AMENDMENT OF PLEADINGS—If the amendment is contested the Master will place the matter in the Court list. Where an order is made by the Master it will specify a time limit for the delivery of the amended pleadings.

N.A.C.

O.63,
r.1(15)

ORDER FOR THE CORRECTION OF MINOR CLERICAL ERRORS (e.g. minor mistake in figures on a summary summons or a spelling error). Since the application is not usually on consent, because it is made *ex parte*, the Master will order that the proceedings must be re-served. As to whether the

Summary of the Rules   67

Master may amend a Summary Summons: see chapter
2.

EP.C.

O.63,
r.1(16)

ORDER TO RECEIVE A CONSENT INTO COURT AND TO MAKE
THE SAME A RULE OF COURT WHERE THE PARTIES ARE *SUI
JURIS* (e.g. consent by a defendant to judgment being en-
tered against him on foot of a summary summons).

EP.

O.63,
r.1(17)

ORDER UNDER THE BANKERS BOOKS EVIDENCE ACTS (see
chapter 3).

EP.G.

O.63,
r.1(18)

ORDER FOR PAYMENT OUT OF FUNDS STANDING TO THE
CREDIT OF AN INFANT—Payment out on attaining majority
no longer requires an application to the Master and can be
done by filing the requisite affidavit in the Central office.
Payments out for the benefit of an infant during his minority
will be made by order of the Master, where the Court Order
directing the funds to be held for the benefit of the infant
directs that such applications be made to him. Otherwise
the application must be made to a Judge (see O. 63, r.12 for
application to have monies paid out during infancy).

EP

O.63,
r.1(19)

ORDER TO HAVE AN ACCOUNT TAKEN OR AN INQUIRY
MADE—The Master will only make such an order in uncontested cases.

N.A.C.

O.63,
r.1(20)

ORDER GIVING LIBERTY TO ISSUE, FOR SERVICE OUTSIDE
THE JURISDICTION, A CITATION TO SEE PROCEEDINGS IN
CONTENTIOUS PROBATE MATTERS—A citation to see pro-

ceedings is issued against all persons to whom administration would be granted in the case of the deceased's
intestacy. It is also issued by a next-of-kin opposing a will
against all persons interested in it.

EP

O.63,
r.1(21)

ORDER GIVING LIBERTY TO ISSUE A CITATION TO LODGE A
GRANT OF PROBATE OR LETTER OF ADMINISTRATION IN
COURT

EP

O.63,
r.1(22)

LIBERTY TO FILE A SUPPLEMENTAL AFFIDAVIT OF SCRIPTS

N.A.G.

O.63,
r.1(23)

LODGMENT OF SCRIPTS BY ANY PARTY

N.A.G.

O.63,
r.1(24)

APPOINTMENT OF A SUBSTITUTE RECEIVER—This rule
applies where the original receiver has died or been discharged. Application should also be made for any
necessary consequential directions as to the accounts of the
original receiver.

N.A.G.

O.63,
r.1(25)

O.46
r.14-18

STOP ORDERS ON MONIES OR SECURITIES IN COURT—The
applicant for such order is a person with a derivative
interest in monies or securities lodged in Court. An order
made under this rule has the effect of staying the transfer,
sale, payment or other disposition of the funds or securities
in Court until such time as the applicant can bring proceedings to establish his claim.

EP.G

<table>
<tr><td>O.63,
r.1(26)</td><td>LIBERTY TO ISSUE A SUBPOENA DUCES TECUM ON A PUBLIC OFFICIAL—i.e. a subpoena for the production of any record in the custody of the Paymaster General or other officer of the State. Generally a subpoena is required to direct a witness to appear in court, but no order is required, except where the witness is in the employment of the Collector General.</td></tr>
</table>

EP.

<table>
<tr><td>O.63,
r.1(27)</td><td>ORDER FOR THE ISSUE OF A CITATION IN A MATRIMONIAL CAUSE OR MATTER—A petitioner in Matrimonial Proceedings is obliged, once he has filed a petition and affidavit to extract such sealed citation for service upon the respondent calling him to appear before the Court to make answer to the Petition.</td></tr>
</table>

EP.C. Draft Citation (Form 2 App L)

<table>
<tr><td>O.63,
r.1(28)</td><td>A SEVEN-DAY ORDER FOR THE PAYMENT OF TAXED COSTS OR LODGMENT OR SECURITY IN MATRIMONIAL PROCEEDINGS—Under O.70, r.77, once the Taxing Master has signed a certificate of taxation or as to security it may be lodged in the Central office and the Master is obliged to issue an order for payment of the amount or the giving of security within seven days.</td></tr>
</table>

N.A.G. (exhibit Taxing Master's cert.)

<table>
<tr><td>O.63,
r.1(29)</td><td>ORDER TO VACATE A LIS PENDENS—Such application is made by the person who registered the *lis pendens*. This must be on consent, if not the party seeking to vacate a lis pendens must apply to the High Court.
N.A. (and certificate of the registration of the *lis pendens*)</td></tr>
</table>

<table>
<tr><td>O.63,
r.1(30)</td><td>ORDER SETTLING THE ISSUES TO BE TRIED UNDER O.33, R.1—The Master may only make such an order on consent,</td></tr>
</table>

settling the issues of fact to be tried where those issues are not sufficiently defined by the pleadings.

N.A.C.G.

O.63, r.1(31)

LIBERTY TO ISSUE EXECUTION IN THE NAME OF OR AGAINST THE LEGAL REPRESENTATIVE OF A DECEASED PARTY INCLUDING THE ISSUE OF ANY EXECUTION PROCESS AGAINST SUCH REPRESENTATIVE UNDER O.42 RR.1-11—Such an order must be secured before an execution order will be issued by the Central Office in the name of or against a personal representative.

N.A.C.G.

O.63, r.1(32)

LIBERTY TO RENEW OR REPLACE AN ORDER OF FIERI FACIAS WITH A NEW ORDER—Such an application is necessary if the original order has either lapsed (after one year) or has been lost.

N.A.G.

O.63, r.1(33)

TRANSFER OF PROCEEDINGS FROM THE HIGH COURT TO THE CIRCUIT OR DISTRICT COURTS—The Master will only make such an order on consent of all the parties. If the transfer is opposed, the matter will be heard by the High Court by motion on notice. The Master has no jurisdiction of his own motion to transfer proceedings—see *De La Hunt v Laffan* [1927] IR 346.

N.A.C.G.

O.63, r.1(24)

LIBERTY TO SERVE A THIRD-PARTY NOTICE—The Master will only make such an order on the consent of the plaintiff. If the plaintiff does not consent, the motion must be brought before the High Court (see O.16).

N.A.C.G.

O.63, r.2   ASSESSMENT OF DAMAGES AND TAKE AN ACCOUNT—The Master will only undertake such an assessment by order of the High Court or on consent of all parties concerned. (see O.13, r.6, O.27, r.8, O.36, rr.43-49, O.41, r.13, O.64, r.46). Damages may be assessed by the Master where the Court has already given judgment e.g. in default of defence, and has ordered that the Master assesses damages. see *Matheson and others v Wilson* [1929] IR 134; and *Dunlop Pneumatic Tyre Co. Ltd v New Garage and Motor Co. Ltd* [1913] 2 KB 207.

N.A.

O.63, r.3   TRIAL OF FACT—On consent of all the parties concerned in proceedings the Master may try any issue of fact.

N.A.C.G.

O.63, r.5   SUPPLEMENTARY OR ANCILLARY JURISDICTION—This rule gives the Master jurisdiction to make any supplementary or ancillary order and give any necessary directions in any matter in which he may make an order under the Rules.

O.63, r.6   THE MASTER HAS A DISCRETION WHETHER TO MAKE AN ORDER FOR COSTS IN ANY MATTER BEFORE HIM—The usual practice is to reserve costs to the trial of the action where the application is an interlocutory one.

O.63, r.7   THE MASTER IS GIVEN A DISCRETION TO TRANSFER ANY CASE BEFORE HIM TO THE COURT LISTS FOR HEARING—He may do so if:
    (a) there is a serious dispute between the parties; or,
    (b) on the application or request of one or all parties.

O.63, r.8   THE MASTER IS GIVEN POWERS SIMILAR TO THOSE OF THE HIGH COURT FOR THE PURPOSE OF ANY CAUSE OR MATTER WITHIN HIS JURISDICTION—This rule states that the Master has power to summons parties and witnesses, administer oaths, take affidavits, affirmations and acknowledgments, require the production of documents and examine parties and witnesses, either upon interrogatories or *viva voce*. Penalties for non compliance with an order of the Master are similar to the High Court (see O.44 for attachment and contempt).

O.63, r.9   APPEAL—An appeal may be taken from any order of the Master (including an order as to costs) to the High Court to discharge the order or make the order refused.

Such appeal must be made within six days of the date of perfection of the Masters order (i.e.the date on which the order is signed by the Masters registrar). If the original application was made *ex parte* ,the appeal must be made within six days from notice of the same or in the case of a refusal, from the date of the refusal.

It may also be possible to judicially review a decision of the Master—see chapter 1

O.63, r.10   ANY ORDER WHICH MAY BE MADE BY THE MASTER MAY BE MADE BY A DEPUTY MASTER—See chapter 1.

O.63, r.11   CERTIFYING FOR COUNSEL—Although counsel may be heard in any application before the Master, the costs of such counsel will not be allowed unless certified for by the Master.

O.63, r.12   APPLICATION FOR PAYMENT OUT OF FUNDS HELD FOR THE BENEFIT OF AN INFANT—This must be made either on affidavit by the infant, the next friend of the infant or the solicitor acting on behalf of the infant; or by letter in writing by the infant, the next friend of the infant or the solicitor acting on behalf of the infant. On such application the Master may make such an order as appears proper, without the need for an *ex parte* application. It is necessary to satisfy the Master that the payment is for the benefit of the infant. Before making the order, the Master may at his discretion having regard to the amount involved or for any other reason which appears to him sufficient make inquiries or raise queries. He may also require the application to be made *ex parte* on the affidavit grounding the application.

E.G.

O.64   ORDER 64 GOVERNS PRACTICE AND PROCEDURE IN ADMIRALTY ACTIONS—The Master has considerable jurisdiction in this area. The Admiralty Judge appointed to hear such actions is a judge of the High Court appointed by the President of the High Court from time to time.

ADMIRALTY ACTIONS IN REM

O.64, r.6   **A. Warrant**

A warrant for the arrest of a ship or other property will be issued under seal by the Master, on the application of either the plaintiff or the defendant, made at any time after the summons is issued. The following steps must be taken when making an application for such warrant—

(a) An application must be filed stating the name and description of the applicant party, the nature of his claim/counterclaim, a description of the property to be arrested and that the claim has not been satisfied.

(b) The applicants solicitor must lodge a written undertaking to pay the fees and expenses of the officer executing the warrant.

(c) In the following cases, the affidavit must contain additional information unless the requirements are waived by the Admiralty judge—

(1) Action for wages or possession—The affidavit must state the nationality of the vessel and if foreign, that notice of the action has been given to that State's representative, if any resides in Dublin and such notice should be annexed to the affidavit.

(2) Action of bottomry—This type of action is no longer common. A bottomry bond is a contract under which the master of a vessel pledges the keel or the bottom of his ship as security for repayment of a loan taken in circumstances of unforseen need or distress, e.g. for urgent repairs. If the vessel returns safely, the lender may bring an action in rem to recover the loan with interest. The bottomry bond and a translation if necessary, must be produced for inspection and perusal by the Master and a certified copy must be annexed to the affidavit.

(3) Action of distribution of salvage—the affidavit must state the amount of salvage awarded or agreed and the name, address and description of the person holding the salvage.

B. Service

Service of the warrant will not be required where the defendant's solicitor agrees to accept service and gives a written undertaking to enter an appearance and to put in bail or money into Court in lieu of bail.If such acceptance is not made, then the warrant of arrest must be served by the officer of the High Court described as the Admiralty Marshall (this position is filled by a registrar of the High Court serving in the Central Office and appointed by the Chief Registrar from time to time. It is an administrative position) or his substitutes in the following manner—

O.64, r.10   (a) Against ship freight or cargo on board. By nailing the original warrant or summons for a short time to the mast or other conspicuous part of the vessel and upon its removal, replacing it with a true copy.

O.64, r.11   (b) Against landed or transhipped cargo. By affixing the original warrant or summons to the cargo for a short time and upon its removal, replacing it with a true copy.

O.64, r.12   If the cargo is in the custody of a person who denies access to it then service may be made upon such person.

O.64, r.18   If property is arrested by such warrant, then it may only be released by order of the Master (rr.26-32 provide for a *caveat* procedure which may be adopted to prevent arrest or release of property, with penalties as to costs if the procedure is abused.) An order for release may be made by the Master if:—

O.64, r.19   (a) the party at whose instance the property was arrested files a notice that he withdraws the warrant before an appearance has been entered, or,

(b) the debt in respect of which proceedings were brought is paid, together with a sum for costs as fixed by the Master, *and*,

(c) an affidavit of value is filed if necessary (see rr.21-22)

O.64, r.45   This rule provides that professional, merchant and other scientific assistance may be sought by the Master and the Master may act upon the certificate of such persons.

O.64, r.46   This rule applies to references made by the Admiralty Judge to the Master. The same rule governs practice and procedure in a reference made by the Admiralty Judge to another Judge under O.64, r.46.2

O.64, r.46(2)   The claimant must file his claim and grounding affidavits within twelve days of the reference (i.e. the date on which the reference was made) and deliver copies of the reference to the other side. Any counter affidavits must be filed and delivered within twelve days thereafter.

<table><tr><td>O.64,
r.46(3)</td><td>Six days are then allowed for any further affidavits. Application must be made to the Master thereafter, if any party wishes to file a further affidavit.   N.A.C.</td></tr></table>

C. Hearing and judgment

<table><tr><td>O.64,
r.46(4)</td><td>The claimant must file a notice requesting that the reference be listed for hearing within three days of the time allowed for the filing of the last affidavit. Failure to do so may lead to the claim being dismissed with costs.</td></tr><tr><td>O.64,
r.46(8)</td><td>The arrangement and hearing of the reference is wholly subject to the control and direction of the Master.</td></tr><tr><td>O.64,
r.46(5)</td><td>Oral evidence may be adduced at the hearing of the reference and the Master will take a note of the evidence unless either party applies for it to be taken down by a shorthand writer (see O.123, r.2).</td></tr><tr><td>O.64, r.48</td><td>All or any of the evidence in Admiralty proceedings may, if so ordered, be given by affidavit.</td></tr><tr><td>O.64,
r.46(6)</td><td>Counsels costs will not be allowed unless the Master deems the attendance of counsel necessary (see O.63, r.11).</td></tr><tr><td>O.64,
r.46(7)</td><td>The Master may certify what costs of the reference should be allowed and to whom.</td></tr><tr><td>O64,
r.46(9)</td><td>The Master will state the result of his inquiry in a signed certificate, which stands confirmed unless challenged within four days, by service of a High Court notice of motion, seeking to set aside or vary the certificate and setting out the grounds.</td></tr><tr><td>O.64,
r.46(11)</td><td>Once the certificate is confirmed, final judgment may be entered in the Central office.</td></tr><tr><td>O.64, r.51</td><td>The Master will hear objections from any person interested in the proceeds of sale of any property sold by the Admiralty Marshall, to the taxation of the Admiralty Marshall's account of expenses.</td></tr><tr><td>O.64, r.52</td><td>The Master may, if he thinks it reasonable, allow any</td></tr></table>

signed agreement between the parties in Admiralty proceedings to be filed in Court, whereupon it becomes an
Order of Court.

<table>
<tr><td>O.70</td><td align="center">MATRIMONIAL CAUSES OR MATTERS</td></tr>
</table>

O.79, rr. 5 & 6

ORDER FOR THE ISSUE OF A CITATION—See O.63, r.1(27)

O.70, r.26

ALTERATIONS AND AMENDMENTS TO PLEADINGS—The sanction of the Master must be sought before any alteration or amendment is made to pleadings. If such permission is being sought in order to rectify a clerical error, the application may be made *ex parte*. Otherwise, the application must be made on notice.

Clerical error EP.C.
Other N.A.C.

O.70, r.32

APPOINTMENT OF MEDICAL INSPECTORS IN NULLITY PROCEEDINGS—The Master may make such an order, on the application of the petitioner, where the proceedings for nullity are on the ground of impotence or incapacity (O.70, r.32(2)) and shall make such an order, on the application of either party, where the proceedings for nullity are on the grounds of non-consummation due to the wilful refusal of the respondent (O. 70, r.32(4)). Such an order is usually made at the same time and on the same application as an order for directions—see O.36, r.4.

N.C.

Note: Where there has been no appearance, within the time allowed, by the respondent and the Citation endorsed pursuant to O.70, r.11 (Form 3 App L) has been filed, an affidavit of service of the Citation in accordance with Form 4 (App L) must be filed, (O. 70, r.14) and the petitioner may then proceed by filling the motion in the Central Office in lieu of service pursuant to O.70, r.79. A certificate of no appearance will also be required.

O.70A, r.10

SERVICE OF FAMILY LAW PROCEEDINGS—The Master has jurisdiction under this rule to direct service of family law proceedings on any person not already a party in such manner as he shall deem fit and such directions may be given at any stage in the proceedings.

EP.C.

O.70A

TRANSFER OF JUDICIAL SEPARATION PROCEEDINGS FROM THE CIRCUIT COURT TO THE HIGH COURT—The Master may give such directions as to the filing of affidavits, supplemental affidavits and amended pleadings as may be necessary 'as if proceedings had commenced in the High Court', and will if necessary direct the service of a new notice of trial. The additional or amended pleadings must be filed in the Central office with the Master's order and thereafter the proceedings will be listed for hearing in the High Court.

N.A.C.G.

O.81, r.1

THE BILLS OF SALE (IRELAND) ACTS 1879 AND 1883—Under O.81 the Master executes the office of Registrar for the purpose of the Bills of Sale Acts.

O.81, r.2

Upon satisfaction and discharge of a bill of sale, the Master may order that a memorandum of satisfaction be written on a registered copy of the bill of sale. Such an order may be made upon delivery of a requisition signed by a solicitor. The Master must also be provided with a consent signed by the holder of the Bill of Sale, which must be verified by affidavit filed in the Central Office. If such consent is not available, the Master may hear a motion on notice and upon being satisfied that the debt (if any) has been discharged, may order a memorandum of satisfaction to be written on a registered copy of the bill of sale.

N.A.G.

O.97   PARLIAMENTARY ELECTION PETITIONS UNDER THE PAR-
LIAMENTARY ELECTIONS ACT, 1868—Such petitions are heard by a panel of three judges nominated annually by the President of the High Court. The Master deals with the

O.97, r.12   receipt and delivery of such petitions (sends a copy to the returning officer) ensuring that particulars of the names and addresses of the petitioners and the respondents agents have been included. The Master will give the petitioner, respondent and the returning officer at least fifteen days

O.97, r.26   notice of the time and place for the trial of the petition and
O.97, r.42   must also notify the Minister for Finance and the Clerk of the Dáil. The Master may acknowledge a recognizance as security for the costs of the petition under r. 18 and hear an

O.97, r.20   objection to the security provided, subject to an appeal to the High Court within five days thereafter.   N.A.C.G.

O.97,   The hearing may be either upon affidavit or by oral exam-
r.20(2)   ination of witnesses or both. Should the objection be allowed by the Master, he may fix the amount which he deems necessary to make the security sufficient.The sum so fixed must then be lodged within five days of the order.

O.97, r.22   The Master may make an order as to the costs of a hearing under r.20. If no such order is made then the costs are included in the general costs of the petition.

O.97, r.24   The Master makes out the election list which must be kept at the Central office, open for inspection.

O.121, r.9   SERVICE OF ANY PROCESS OR CITATION IN FOREIGN PRO-
CEEDINGS—This Order governs service of documents. If a Court or Tribunal of a foreign country is seeking service of

any process or citation in any civil or commercial matter pending before it on any person in Ireland, a letter of request must first be sent to the Minister for Foreign Affairs. Should the Minister decide that it is desirable to effect such service, he will forward the matter together with an intimation of his views to the Master.

The following documentation must be supplied—

(a) the letter of request and a translation thereof, if necessary

(b) two copies of the process or citation and two translated copies thereof Service must be effected in accordance with O.121, r.9(2)(3).

O.121, r.9(4)

Once served, a copy of the process and an affidavit containing particulars as to the cost of service and duly notarised, must be returned to the Master.

O.121, r.9(5)

The costs must be submitted to taxation.

O.121, r.9(6)

Once service has been effected and the costs thereof taxed, the Master will prepare and transmit to the Minister for foreign affairs, a certificate of service of foreign process. The certificate will be Form 3 (App. D, Part III of the Rules), and the following documentation must be annexed—

a copy of the letter of request; a copy of the process or citation served and evidence of such service, duly notarised; a copy of the charges for service and the Taxing Master's certificate.

O.123, r.2

INQUIRY AS TO DAMAGES OR OTHER PROCEEDINGS— Application may be made under this rule to have proceedings recorded by a shorthand writer appointed by the Master, who will then take a note of the oral evidence and the Master's findings. This is an exception to the normal rule that the Master shall personally take down and preserve the evidence given at the hearing (see O.36, r.44).

Appendix A: Notes on Affidavits

The majority of applications heard by the Master are motions on notice grounded on affidavit. It is therefore essential to comply with the requirements and formalities relating to affidavits as set out in O.40 of the Rules.

All affidavits for use in the Master's Court must be filed in the Central Office before the motion is heard by the Master (O.52, r.16). Notice of any affidavits to be used in support of an application before the Master must be given to the other party (O.40, r.23). If replying or supplementary affidavits have not been filed and notice given prior to an application the Master may adjourn the application. (O.52, r.9).

In affidavits for use in interlocutory motions the deponent may make statements as to his belief and the grounds thereof. In all other matters affidavits must be limited to such facts as the deponent is able to prove of his own knowledge (O.40, r.4).

Affidavits must be drawn up in the first person and divided into paragraphs (O.40, r.8). Every affidavit must be marked with the title of the cause or matter. Every affidavit must commence with the words 'I, A.B. make oath and say. . . .' The affidavit must state the description and residence of the deponent. Affidavits of service must state when, where, and how, and by whom such service was effected. (O.40, r.9).

No interlineations or alterations may be made to an affidavit unless they are authenticated by the initials of the person who administers the oath, and no alterations may be made by erasure (O.40, r.13). See also O.40, r.25, every alteration in an account before the Master must be marked with the initials of the person before whom the affidavit is sworn, and such alterations must not be made by erasure.

A certified copy Affidavit may be used in Court where the original has been filed. It is essential that a true copy of an affidavit should be served on the opposite party. Where the signature of the deponent or the place where the affidavit was sworn was omitted on the copy served, this was held to be a fatal defect—*Best v Woods* 39 ILTR 44. Where a certified copy affidavit is handed in to the Master for the hearing of an application, the same must be an accurate copy (O.40, r.16).

Affidavits must be sworn before a Judge, a Commissioner for Oaths or officer empowered to administer oaths. The majority of affidavits are sworn before Commissioners for Oaths. A Commissioner cannot act in a case involving his own client.

The jurat must certify that the Commissioner knows the deponent or that the deponent has been identified to him. Where an affidavit is being sworn by an illiterate or blind person the Commissioner must certify that the affidavit was read in his presence to the deponent and that the deponent seemed to understand it, that the deponent made his signature or mark in the presence of the Commissioner.

Where affidavits are sworn abroad they may be sworn before Irish diplomatic or consular representative or agent exercising his functions in that country. If there is no such person or if they are not conveniently near to the deponent then the affidavit may be sworn before any notary public lawfully authorised to administer oaths in that country. Where such country is part of the British Commonwealth or a British possession the affidavit may be sworn before any judge, court, notary public or person authorised to administer oaths in such part or possession (see O.40, r.7).

Where an affidavit is sworn abroad it is the practice to accept the signature or seal of any such diplomatic or consular representative or agent, judge, court, notary public or other person. 'Where the person before whom an Affidavit is sworn is neither a judge, notary public, justice of the peace, magistrate nor commissioner for oaths, it is desirable that he should add to his description the words "lawfully authorised to administer oaths".' from *Stringer on Oaths*, 4th ed. at p.70—see *Applebe v Applebe* [1931] IR 286.

On every affidavit there must be a clause showing by whom it was filed. 'Filed this   day of   , by   , Solicitors for the Plaintiff/Defendant' (O.40, r.11).

Appendix B: Special Indorsement of Claim on a Summary Summons[1]

See Appendix A Form 2 and Appendix B Part III (I) of the Rules Samples of Special Indorsements of Claim, Notices of Motion and Grounding Affidavits are set out below.

PART ONE

I: SPECIAL INDORSEMENT OF CLAIM ON FOOT OF A GUARANTEE IN RESPECT OF BANKING FACILITIES

THE PLAINTIFF'S CLAIM is for £   being money due and owing by the Defendant to the Plaintiff under and by virtue of a letter of Guarantee in writing dated the   day of   , whereby the Defendant in consideration of the Plaintiff making or continuing advances or otherwise giving credit or affording banking facilities to XY Company Ltd as long as the Plaintiff should think fit the Defendant agreed to pay to the Plaintiff on demand all sums of money then owing or which at any time be owing or remain unpaid to the Plaintiff anywhere from or by the said XY Company Ltd whether as principal or surety and whether solely or jointly with any other party or from any firm in which the said XY Company Ltd might be a partner, upon current overdraft accounts, promissory notes or bills discounted or paid and other loans, of the said XY Company Ltd solely or jointly or of

---

1. See chapter 2 as to use of summary summonses.

any such firm as aforesaid whether for actual or contingent liability or on any account whatsoever together with all interest discount and other bankers charges including legal charges occasioned by or incident to this or any other security held by or offered to the Plaintiff for the ultimate balance or by or to the enforcement of any such security provided always that the total liability ultimately the sum of £
plus interest from the date of demand or earlier determination of the Guarantee until payment calculated at the Plaintiff bank's ruling rate or rates for overdrawn current accounts compoundable with quarterly rests together with all costs, charges and expenses.[2] A demand for payment was made on the Principal debtor XY Company Ltd on the
         day of   . The said XY Company Ltd was on the
         day of   and still is indebted to the Plaintiff on foot of the accounts at the Plaintiff's branch at   in the City of Dublin in a sum in excess of £   . The Plaintiff demanded payment of the sum of £   from the Defendant on the
      day of   but the Defendant has failed to pay the same or any part thereof to date.

Particulars:

      day of   To amount due as of said date
                          on foot of the said Guarantee of
                          the said Defendant   £

The Plaintiff claims further interest from the   day of
      being the day after the date upon which the Guarantee was called due at current rates until payment or Judgment and the Plaintiff claims the costs of these proceedings.

Signed

      Plaintiff or Solicitors for the Plaintiff

2.   In accordance with the terms of the letter of guarantee.

THE HIGH COURT
(Record No.)

BETWEEN/

A.B.

PLAINTIFF

AND

C.D.

DEFENDANT

NOTICE OF MOTION

TAKE NOTICE that on the   day of   at the hour of 10.30 o'clock in the forenoon or on the first available opportunity thereafter Counsel on behalf of the Plaintiff will apply to the Master of the High Court sitting at the Four Courts, Inns Quay in the City of Dublin for the following relief:

(i) An Order granting the Plaintiff liberty to enter final judgment for the sum of £   [3] together with further interest on the Principal sum £   [4] from   day of   .[5]

(ii) The costs of these proceedings.

WHICH SAID APPLICATION shall be grounded upon the Summary

3. Amount claimed in the special indorsement of claim plus interest to date of swearing of affidavit grounding this motion.
4. Amount claimed in the special indorsement of claim.
5. Date of swearing of affidavit.

Summons herein issued on the   day of   , the
Notice of Entry of Appearance entered thereto on the   day
of   , the Affidavit of E.F. (a copy of which is served
herewith) together with the exhibits therein contained, this Notice of
Motion and the Affidavit of Service hereof, the nature of the case and
the reasons to be offered.

Dated this   day of

Signed

   Solicitors for the Plaintiff
   (address)

To: C.D. or Solicitors for the Defendant
       (address)

And: The Registrar
        Central Office
        Four Courts
        Dublin 7

III: GROUNDING AFFIDAVIT

THE HIGH COURT
(Record No.)

BETWEEN/

A.B.

PLAINTIFF

AND

C.D.

DEFENDANT

AFFIDAVIT OF E.F.

I, E.F., (occupation) of (address) aged 18 years and upwards MAKE OATH and SAY as follows:

1. I am an Officer of the Plaintiff's branch at (address) and I am duly authorised to make this Affidavit. I make this Affidavit from facts within my own knowledge from personal recollection and from the books and records of the Plaintiff branch save where otherwise appears and where so appearing I believe the same to be true.

2. I beg to refer to the particulars endorsed on the Summary Summons herein and to confirm their accuracy. I say that the Defendant is indebted to the Plaintiff on foot of a contract of guarantee. I beg to refer to the said contract of guarantee which was executed on the
day of   and upon which marked with the letter 'A' I have signed my name prior to the swearing hereof. I say that the party whose debts are thereby guaranteed XY Company Ltd was on the
day of   and remains, indebted to the Plaintiff of a sum in excess of £   .[6] I say that on the day of   a letter was sent to XY Company Ltd demanding payment of the said sum of £   . I say that on the   day of   a letter was sent to the Defendant calling upon him to honour the said contract of guarantee. I beg to refer to a copy of the said letters dated
day of   and   day of   upon which pinned together and marked with the letter 'B' I have signed my name prior to the swearing hereof. I say that the Defendant has not honoured the terms of the said contract of guarantee and that the sum of £
[7] remains due and owing to the Plaintiff. I further say that under the terms of the said contract of guarantee the Plaintiff has been entitled to charge interest on the sum of £   from the   day

6.   Amount claimed in the special indorsement of claim.
7.   Amount claimed in the special indorsement of claim.

of   being the day after the date upon which the guarantee
was called.

3. I say that the Plaintiff has calculated interest on the said sum of £
             from the   day of   [8] to the date of
swearing of this affidavit which sum is calculated as follows:

To interest on the principal sum of £
from the   day of   down to
the   day of   at the rate of
% per annum (days)[9]   £

To interest on the principal sum of £
from the day of   down to the   day
of   at the rate of % per annum (days)   £

TOTAL INTEREST DUE   £

4. I say that as of the date of swearing this Affidavit interest in the sum
of £   [10] has accrued. I further say that interest is continuing
to accrue at the rate of   % per annum which represents a daily
accretion of £

5. I say I have been advised by the Plaintiff company's solicitors and
believe that the Defendant has no bona fide defence to the Plaintiff's
claim and the Appearance entered on his behalf has been for the sole
purpose of delay.

6. I therefore pray this Honourable Court for liberty to enter final
judgment for the sum of £   as sought in the Summary

8.   Date on which entitlement to interest arose.
9.   Number of days.
10.   Total interest due.

Summons herein together with interest thereupon as hereinbefore calculated, and for the costs of these proceedings.

Sworn by the said E.F. this   day of
      at   in the City of
before me a Commissioner to Administer Oaths
in the High Court and I know the Deponent

E.F.   G.H.
Commissioner for Oaths

This Affidavit is filed by   Solicitors for the Plaintiff (address)

Filed this   day of

PART TWO

I: SPECIAL INDORSEMENT OF CLAIM[1]

FOR GOODS SOLD AND DELIVERED

THE PLAINTIFF'S CLAIM is for £50,000 being the price of goods sold and delivered by the Plaintiff to the Defendant at the request of the Defendant within the last six years.

Particulars

invoice number	date	amount
001	1.2.91	£10,000.00
002	1.4.91	£10,000.00
003	1.6.91	£10,000.00
004	1.8.91	£10,000.00
005	1.10.91	£10,000.00
		£50,000.00

1. See chapter 2 for details required in special indorsement of claim.

AND THE PLAINTIFF CLAIMS £50,000.00 together with interest thereon pursuant to the Courts Act, 1981 and the costs of these proceedings.

Signed:
> Plaintiff or Solicitors for the Plaintiff
> Address

Where the claim is for a liquidated sum only an indorsement for costs is added—see Order 4 r.5, Form 2 Appendix A and Part III (I) Appendix B of the Rules.

II: MOTION SEEKING LIBERTY TO ENTER FINAL JUDGMENT

THE HIGH COURT
(Record No.)

BETWEEN/

A.B.

PLAINTIFF

AND

C.D.

DEFENDANT

NOTICE OF MOTION

TAKE NOTICE that on the   day of   at the hour of 10.30 o'clock in the forenoon or on the first available opportunity thereafter Counsel on behalf of the Plaintiff herein will apply to the Master of the High Court sitting at the Four Courts, Inns Quay, Dublin 7 for the following relief:

(i) An Order granting the Plaintiff liberty to enter final judgment for the sum of £   together with interest pursuant to the Courts Act,

1981[1] claimed in the Special Indorsement of Claim on the Summary Summons herein;

(ii) The costs of these proceedings.

WHICH SAID APPLICATION will be grounded upon the Summary Summons herein, the Notice of Entry of Appearance herein, the affidavit of E.F. (a copy of which is served herewith) together with the exhibits therein contained, this Notice of Motion and the Affidavit of Service hereof, the nature of the case and the reasons to be offered.

Dated this   day of

Signed
            Solicitors for the Plaintiff
            (address)

To: C.D. or Solicitors for the Defendant[2]
            (address)

And: The Registrar
            Central Office
            Four Courts
            Dublin 7
Grounding affidavit of E.F.

---

1.   The master may not grant interest pursuant to the Courts Act, 1981 — see Chapter 2.
2.   If the defendant has solicitors on record the motion is served on that firm.

III: GROUNDING AFFIDAVIT

THE HIGH COURT
(Record No)

BETWEEN/

A.B.

PLAINTIFF

AND

C.D.

DEFENDANT

AFFIDAVIT OF E.F.

I, E.F. (occupation) of (address) aged 18 years and upwards MAKE OATH and say as follows:

1. I am employed by the Plaintiff Company as a Book-keeper and I make this Affidavit for and on behalf of the Plaintiff's and I am duly authorised to do so. I beg to refer to the Summary Summons herein and to the Special Indorsement of Claim thereon when produced.

2. I make this Affidavit from facts within my own knowledge from personal recollection and from the books and records of the Plaintiff Company save where otherwise appears and whereso appearing I believe the same to be true.

3. The Plaintiff Company has its registered office at (address).

4. The Plaintiff Company carries on a business inter alia in (type of business) and the Defendant herein was at all material times in receipt of the Plaintiff Company's products.

5. I say that in February, April, June, August and October 1991 the Plaintiff Company sold and delivered goods to the value of £50,000.00

to the Defendant and that the Defendant paid no sum whatsoever to the Plaintiff in respect of the said sales. I say that there is the sum of £50,000.00 due and owing to the Plaintiff from the Defendant and I say that the said sum is rightly due and owing by the Defendant to the Plaintiff over and above all just credits and allowances. I beg to refer to copies of invoices and to a statement of account upon which pinned together and marked with the letter 'A' I have signed my name prior to the swearing hereof.

6. I say that I have been advised by the Plaintiff Company's solicitors and believe that the Defendant has no bona fide defence either at law or on the merits to the Plaintiff's claim and the appearance entered on his behalf has been entered for the sole purpose of delay.

7. I therefore pray this Honourable Court for liberty to enter final judgment for the sum of £   and for the costs of these proceedings.

                           Sworn by the said E.F. this   day of
                                  at   in the City of
                           before me a Commissioner to Administer Oaths
                           in the High Court and I know the Deponent

Signature of E.F.   G.H.
                         Commissioner for Oaths

This Affidavit is filed on behalf of the Plaintiff by Messrs (name of firm) Solicitors of (address)

Filed this   day of

Appendix C: Documents Needed to Enter Final Judgment

Where leave to enter final judgment is granted by the Master the Plaintiff proceeds to enter judgment in the Central Office

To do so he will require:

(a) The Master's order bespoken from the Central Office

(b) Judgment form

(c) A supplemental affidavit may be required if there is additional (contract) interest.

Where no appearance has been entered the plaintiff proceeds to obtain judgment in the Central Office.

To do so he will require a set of papers as set out in chapter 2.

(a) Summary summons

(b) Affidavit of service

(c) Affidavit of debt

(d) Judgment form

A. SUMMARY SUMMONS WITH SPECIAL ENDORSEMENT OF CLAIM

See Appendix B.

B. AFFIDAVIT OF SERVICE

THE HIGH COURT
(Record No.)

BETWEEN/

A.B.

PLAINTIFF

AND

C.D.

DEFENDANT

AFFIDAVIT OF SERVICE[1]

I, L.M. (occupation) of (address) aged 18 years and upwards MAKE OATH and say as follows:

1. I say that on   day of   at (address of post office) that I did serve the above named Defendant by posting to them in a pre-paid envelope addressed to them at their registered office at (address), a true copy of the Summary Summons in the above entitled proceedings issued under Seal of the High Court and dated the day of   and marked (record no) upon which said Summons and copy the required Memorandum and Indorsements were duly subscribed and made.

2. I further say that I did afterwards on   day of (being within three days after the service aforesaid) indorse the said Summons the day of the week and the month of such service.

---

1.   See Appendix A and O.40 r.9 of the Rules. This will vary depending on the method of service and on whether it is served on the respondent personally or on his solicitors.

Sworn by the said L.M. this day of
at   in the City of   before
me a Commissioner to Administer Oaths and I
know the Deponent

Signed by L.M.   R.S.
                      Commissioner for Oaths

This Affidavit is filed on behalf of the Plaintiff by Messrs (name of firm) Solicitors of (address)

Filed this   day of

C. AFFIDAVIT OF DEBT

THE HIGH COURT
(Record No.)

BETWEEN/

A.B.

PLAINTIFF

AND

C.D.

DEFENDANT

AFFIDAVIT OF E.F.

I, E.F. (occupation) of (address) aged 18 years and upwards MAKE OATH and say as follows:

1. I am employed by the Plaintiff Company as a Book-keeper and I make this Affidavit for and on behalf of the Plaintiff's and with its authority. I say that the sum of £50,000.00 being the price of goods sold and delivered by the Plaintiff to the Defendant being the sum for which the Plaintiff seeks Judgment is now actually due by the Defendant to the Plaintiff over and above all just and fair allowances.

2. I make this Affidavit from facts within my own knowledge from personal recollection and from the books and records of the Plaintiff Company.

        Sworn by the said E.F. this day of
        at   in the City of   before
        me a Commissioner to Administer Oaths in the
        High Court and I know the Deponent

Signature of E.F.   R.S.
        Commissioner for Oaths

This Affidavit is filed on behalf of the Plaintiff by Messrs (name of firm) Solicitors of (address)

Filed this   day of

D. JUDGMENT FORM

THE HIGH COURT
(Record No.)

BETWEEN/

A.B.

having their registered offices at (adddress)
a Limited Liability Company

PLAINTIFF

AND

C.D.

having their registered offices at (address)
a Limited Liability Company

DEFENDANT

We hereby certify that the Decree, Quality, Profession or Trade and Place of Residence of each of the parties to this Judgment are correctly stated above, and the necessary Affidavits having been filed, we require Judgment to be marked.

Dated   day of

Signed
        Solicitors for the Plaintiff
        (address)

Appendix D: Notice of Motion[1]

THE HIGH COURT
(Record No)

BETWEEN/

A.B.

PLAINTIFF

AND

C.D.

DEFENDANT

NOTICE OF MOTION

TAKE NOTICE that on the   day of   at the hour of 10.30 o'clock in the forenoon or on the first available opportunity thereafter Counsel on behalf of the Plaintiff/Defendant[2] will apply to the Master of the High Court sitting at the Four Courts, Inns Quay in the City of Dublin for the following relief:

(a)   an order pursuant to Order Rule of the Rules of the Superior Courts directing.............[3]

---

1. See Chapter 5 as to when notices of motion are required.
2. Delete as appropriate—for whichever party is making the application.
3. E.g. an order for discovery pusuant to O.31 r.12(1) directing that (any other party) make discovery on oath of the documents which are or have been in his possession or power, relating to the matter in question (see Chapter 3).

(b) the costs of this application.

WHICH SAID APPLICATION shall be grounded upon the proceedings already had herein,[4] this notice of motion, the affidavit of
service hereof, the nature of the case and the reasons to be offered.
   If the motion is to be grounded on affidavit this paragraph should
be substituted as follows:

WHICH SAID APPLICATION shall be grounded upon the proceedings already had herein, the Affidavit of E.F. (a copy of which is
served herewith) together with the exhibits therein contained, this
notice of motion and the affidavit of service hereof, the nature of the
case and the reasons to be offered.

Dated this   day of

Signed
            Applicant or Solicitors for the (Applicant)

To: Respondent or Solicitors for the (Respondent)

& To: The Registrar
         Central Office
         Four Courts
         Dublin 7

4.   E.g. the plenary summons, statement of claim, defence etc.
5.   Depending on whether the applicant is represented by a firm of solicitors.
6.   Depending on whether the respondent has a firm of solicitors acting on his behalf.

Index